Selection post-16:
the role of examination results

SCHOOLS COUNCIL EXAMINATIONS
BULLETIN 45

Selection post-16:
the role of examination results

report of the Uses Made of Examination Results Project

BRIAN GOACHER

Methuen Educational

This title, an outcome of work done for the Schools Council before its closure, is published under the aegis of the School Curriculum Development Committee, Newcombe House, 45 Notting Hill Gate, London W11 3JB

*First published 1984
by Methuen Educational
11 New Fetter Lane, London EC4P 4EE*

© *Schools Council Publications 1984*

All rights reserved. No part of this book may be reprinted or reproduced or utilized in any form or by any electronic, mechanical or other means, now known or hereafter invented, including photocopying and recording, or in any information storage or retrieval system, without permission in writing from the publishers.

*Filmset in Monophoto Times by
Northumberland Press Ltd, Gateshead
Printed in Great Britain by
Richard Clay (The Chaucer Press) Ltd
Bungay, Suffolk*

British Library Cataloguing in Publication Data

Goacher, Brian
Selection post-16.—(Schools Council examinations bulletin; 45)
1. Colleges and universities—Entrance requirements—England   2. Recruiting of employees —Great Britain
I. Title   II. Series
378'.6'64   LB2351

ISBN 0–423–51300–1

Contents

	Foreword	7
	Acknowledgements	9
I	**Setting the scene**	11
	Evolution and adaptation: the development of public examinations	12
	Research and development: evaluation and change	17
	The changing climate	24
	Methods	26
	The sample	27
	Summary and matters arising	29
II	**The use made of 16+ examinations**	31
	Range of provision	31
	Conditions applied to course entry	34
	Full-time non-advanced courses other than GCE	51
	Entry to higher education	55
	Employers and public examinations at 16+	56
	Summary and discussion	63
III	**The use made of 18+ examinations**	68
	Range of provision	69
	Number of applicants and size of course	71
	Information about applicants	75
	Interviewing	79
	Conditions applied to course entry	81
	Admission to Oxford and Cambridge	91
	Employers and public examinations at 18+	93
	Summary and discussion	95

IV	**Users' views of examinations and some alternatives**	98
	Knowledge of the system of examinations	98
	The present system of examining at 16+	99
	The present system of examining at 18+	110
	Summary and discussion	113
V	**Implications for the future**	115
	A review of some of the issues	116
	Making better use of examinations	127
	Suggestions for teachers and educational institutions	127
	Suggestions for local government administrators, advisers and inspectors	129
	Suggestions for central government	129
	Suggestions for examining boards	130
	Suggestions for users of examination results	131
	Appendices	133
	A Project information	135
	B Admissions to Oxford and Cambridge	141
	C Material collected in the course of the Project	153
	D Background information	160
	Bibliography	163
	Members of the Monitoring and Review Group	171

Foreword

In 1980 the Schools Council initiated five three-year programmes of work. Programme 5 – Improving the Examinations System – was unusual in incorporating the Council's statutory examinations responsibilities and also launching enquiries into several key assessment matters.

Work has naturally concentrated on examinations developments at 16+, 17+ and 18+, but there have also been studies of ways of reporting constructively on a wider range of pupil achievement.

Within the past two years the programme has generated a considerable number of reviews, bulletins and research studies on topics as diverse as graded tests, coursework in English, pupil profiles and differentiated examinations. Each publication has sought to explore salient ideas and provide up-to-date information for those concerned with making policy and those charged with putting it into effect.

In many ways the present investigation provides a backdrop against which other, more specific studies can be viewed. The work was mounted in a climate of concern that public examination results do not adequately provide the sort of information needed by employers and admissions tutors when they select applicants for jobs and courses. Anecdotal evidence suggested that selectors were not satisfied with the type of information associated with GCE and CSE examination results. In some cases it was clear that 'users' were implementing their own assessment devices to supplement – and even replace – the usual school qualifications and references. Often, it was claimed that new systems – including criterion-referenced tests and pupil profiles – would provide more appropriate evidence of the required intellectual and personal qualities. However, there had been few recent systematic enquiries capable of throwing light on users' views and procedures.

This report is the outcome of a two-year study of the uses made of examination results by selectors for the full range of post-16 institutions and many sectors of employment. The fact that it has come to fruition is a testament to the energy and skill of Brian Goacher and project assistant Joan Leake. Mr Goacher took over the project in its final phase and has created a full and informative picture of current practice and opinion. There are important lessons in these pages for all who have responsibility for reporting on pupils' attainments and all who use such evidence to select recruits. The Council is most grateful to Brian Goacher for his valuable report.

Like other Programme 5 projects, this work was overseen by the Monitoring and Review Group set up for this purpose by the Council's Examinations Committee. The membership of the Group is given on page 171.

KEITH WELLER
Principal Educational Adviser
Schools Council

Acknowledgements

When a project has spread its net so wide and involved so many individuals and organizations, it is difficult to do justice to the richness and variety of the many contributions.

Judy Dean and Jenny Kennedy were both Project leaders at critical phases of the research and both left their mark upon what was accomplished. Joan Leake remained as project assistant to the very end and without the continuity which she provided, this report could never have been completed.

Warm thanks are also due to Janet Jones, who made available information collected during her time as BP Research Fellow at Reading University School of Education, and was always willing to discuss the wider implications. Her work allowed employers to be represented and without her efforts the report would have offered a far less comprehensive picture of practice. The support of Professor Jack Wrigley in this connection is also much appreciated.

The guidance and support of the Project Steering Group – David Clemson, Lesley Kant, Lea Orr and Keith Weller – were invaluable during the preparation of this account. I would also like to record my appreciation of the interest taken in the report by the members of the Monitoring and Review Group, who are named at the end of this book.

Finally, the many hours devoted by those from all sectors of education and from the examinations system demands acknowledgement. Without their interest and their professional contributions, nothing could have been accomplished.

BRIAN GOACHER
Project Leader

I. Setting the scene

Public examinations at 16 + and 18 + remain the only demonstration of accountability common to all secondary schools. This report is the account of an exploration of the uses to which the results of examinations are put. It attempts to bring together information from a wide variety of sources and to present it in a form which makes it accessible. It is hoped that the report will offer insights and point to ways in which the system might be developed.

The Uses Made of Examination Results Project, which started in January 1981, formed part of the Schools Council's Programme 5 activities aimed at 'improving the examinations system'. Within the Programme the Project complemented a wide range of other activities which included the monitoring of examinations, research on examination strategies, alternatives to examining, development work on examining in a multicultural society and studies of fourth-year options.

While examinations are a subject about which almost everyone is ready to express an opinion, they are seen at one extreme as guardians of standards and identified at the other as alien and malevolent intruders upon the educational scene. Rising youth unemployment, reductions in the number of university places, initiatives from the Manpower Services Commission (MSC), long-standing attempts to reform the system of examinations at 16+ and 18+ and the more recent proposals for reform at 17+ have added further dimensions and increased the complexity of the area. The slow pace and cyclical nature of change which characterizes our education system has also ensured that many existing examinations structures were formed in very different circumstances while the debates which led to their introduction remain familiar.

Roach (1971) identifies the nineteenth-century origins of examinations and points to the speed with which growth took place:

Public examinations were one of the great discoveries of nineteenth century Englishmen. Almost unknown at the beginning of the century, they rapidly became a major tool of social policy. They were used to recruit men for government service, they selected the ablest students in the universities, they controlled the work of the secondary schools, they were used by the State to regulate grants to elementary education ...

Like many 'discoveries', examinations were not new nor were the purposes to which they were put. Their development was not received uncritically and it is almost impossible to discover any aspect of examining which has not been the subject of repeated discussion over the years. The emphasis might change, priorities might alter, but the key questions are repeatedly reset in contexts which reflect the concerns of the moment.

As examinations became established the initial debates tended to focus upon political issues concerned with control and centralization. By the beginning of the twentieth century discussion increasingly centred upon professional aspects of examining such as statistics and techniques of educational measurement. Within the past three or four decades examination issues have often been presented in sociological terms. It is worth noting that some who gave evidence to the Project considered that the focus of the debate had most recently returned to those very political considerations which had been of concern one hundred years before.

Before exploring recent examinations research and describing the methods adopted for the present study, three recurring issues – diversity, impact and control – will be used to provide the framework for a brief discussion of the development of public examinations.

Evolution and adaptation: the development of public examinations

THE DIVERSITY OF PROVISION

Many bodies offering examinations to schools and colleges have their origin in the nineteenth century. The locally taken examinations introduced from 1857 by Oxford and Cambridge Universities and by the College of Preceptors were such powerful instruments of influence within education, and proved to be so financially profitable, that they were quickly copied. The current university involvement in public examinations in the schools was virtually fully developed by 1911. This provision of school examinations was mirrored by the development of examinations for those attending Mechanics Institutes.*

---

* The Union of Lancashire and Cheshire Institutes, the Royal Society of Arts, the City and Guilds of London Institute, the London Chamber of Commerce, Pitman's College and the Union of Educational Institutes all date from this period and many were subsequently responsible for 'filling the gap' in examination provision which emerged after the implementation of the 1944 Education Act.

The dangers of uncoordinated growth were quickly recognized:

The existing multiplicity of external examinations, the claims of which at present so frequently interfere with the best work of the schools, should be reduced by concerted action (Board of Education, 1911).

The problem was resolved, albeit temporarily, by the creation of the Secondary Schools Examinations Council (SSEC) and by the granting of official recognition to only two school examinations after 1917 – the School Certificate and the Higher School Certificate. These 'grouped' examinations, where passes in several specified subjects were required before the awarding of a certificate, remained a major influence in secondary education until they were replaced by single-subject General Certificate of Education examinations at 'Ordinary' and 'Advanced' levels in 1951/53 (GCE O and A levels).*

The replacement was largely a reaction to mounting criticism of the nature of grouped examinations, but the introduction of single subjects and the increasing proportion of pupils remaining within secondary schools led to a further expansion inside and outside the GCE sector.

The case for rationalization of 16 + examinations other than GCE was made forcibly in the Beloe Report (Ministry of Education, 1958):

... the very fact that the GCE has come to be regarded, at 'O' level as at 'A' level, as the passport to higher education or professional status or at least to the better paid posts, has resulted in the examinations at 'O' level attracting a steadily increasing number of entries from institutions other than grammar schools ... The GCE examination, although it attracts large and growing numbers, is by and large regarded by teachers and parents as suitable only for a strictly limited proportion of pupils ... There has been in consequence a mounting demand from teachers, parents and pupils alike for examinations of a different kind and less exacting standard ... In response to this demand there has been a rapid and variegated growth of examinations ...

The report went on to identify four main categories of examination arising from this demand† and to provide a critique of these examinations and their effect upon pupils, teachers and the curriculum. The unsatisfactory nature of marking arrangements, the narrowness of the syllabuses, a concentration of questions upon 'memorized facts and opinions' and the

---

* The present GCE Examining Bodies are listed in Appendix D.
† These were local examinations, school examinations conducted by bodies with regional or national coverage, further education examinations and specialist examinations. Only the first had Ministry approval.

14 SETTING THE SCENE

lack of a 'distinctive aim' were criticized and the report urged rationalization.

The Beloe Report recommendations were given a practical framework in 1962 with the publication of the Fifth Report of the Secondary School Examinations Council (SSEC, 1962a); this subsequently received government approval. Fourteen new regional examining bodies for the Certificate of Secondary Education (CSE) were established and candidates took the first examination in 1965.*

Like GCE, the new system was a single-subject examination. A five-grade marking system was established and the standard of achievement was tied to O-level grades:

In each subject the examination should be so constructed that a sixteen year old pupil whose ability in the subject is such that he might reasonably have secured a pass in Ordinary level of the GCE examination, had he applied himself to a course of study leading to that examination, may reasonably expect to secure Grade 1 in the CSE examination having applied himself to a course of study regarded by teachers of the subject as appropriate to his age, ability and aptitude (SSEC, 1962a).

This equivalence was checked in a monitoring exercise carried out by the National Foundation for Educational Research (NFER) in 1965 and repeated in each of the four subsequent years.

Although the creation of CSE led to a dramatic reduction in the types of examination used by schools, the single-subject nature of both 16 + examinations, the range of modes of examining and the growth in examination board numbers gave rise to new forms of diversity and new problems of comparability. Comparability assumed a new importance within subjects, between subjects, over time and in relationships between examinations at 16 + and 18 +.

THE IMPACT OF EXAMINATIONS

Because the majority of timed written examinations place emphasis upon the recall of information, they inevitably have a profound effect upon course content. Examiners may seek to concern themselves with understanding, synthesis, extrapolation and originality, but it is the traditional emphasis which has led to much dissatisfaction.

The 1911 Consultative Committee, for example, while professing the conviction that external examinations were desirable in secondary schools,

---

* The CSE Examining Bodies, and the other major examining and validating bodies, are listed in Appendix D.

provided a summary of the good and bad effects of examinations which so retained its value over time that it was reproduced in full in the Beloe Report (Ministry of Education, 1958). Some of the effects detailed were concerned with the training value of 'getting up of a subject for a definite purpose' (identified as valuable preparation for lawyers, administrators, journalists and those in business), but most dealt with the impact of examinations upon the curriculum and with how pupils were taught.

Many of the same caveats were repeated by the Spens Committee (Board of Education, 1938), who recorded that:

despite all safeguards the Schools Certificate Examination ... now dominates the work of the schools, controlling both the framework and the content of the curriculum.

Further concerns were detailed in the Norwood Report (Board of Education, 1943):

[the School Certificate] Examination dictates the curriculum and it cannot be otherwise; it confines experiment, limits free choice and subject, hampers treatment of subjects, encourages wrong values in the classroom.

Norwood went on to make radical recommendations for reform. The group nature of the examination was particularly felt to impose undesirable limitations upon the curriculum of individual schools.

Still more pressure for reform can be found in the First Report of the Secondary School Examinations Council (SSEC, 1947), which recommended that greater attention be paid to internal school examinations and school reports. It also proposed a single-subject examination to liberate the curriculum and allow pupils to obtain credit for any satisfactory performance. This change represented an important rejection of the 'hurdle' principle that had hitherto dominated examinations and introduced a credit model where greater emphasis was placed upon success.

It was also suggested that the Ordinary-level papers should be limited to pupils over the age of 16 and designed:

to provide a reasonable test in the subject for pupils who have taken it as a part of a wide and general secondary course up to the age of ... 16, or for pupils who have taken the subject in a non-specialist way in the sixth form.

It was suggested that the Advanced-level examination papers to replace the Higher School Certificate should offer: 'A reasonable test in the subject for pupils who have taken it as a specialist subject for two years of sixth form study'.

Of particular relevance to the current study, a further 'Scholarship' (S) level of examination was outlined which was designed to assist with selection for university entrance and which would offer:

ample choice of questions not necessarily covering a substantially wider field of study than those in the 'Advanced' papers to give specially gifted pupils an opportunity for showing distinctive merit and promise.*

Because all these examinations were identified as qualifying examinations it was further suggested that only pass/fail grading should be used, although, to permit those taking an A-level subject to bypass the examination at O level, it was recommended that there should be a provision for awarding O-level passes on A-level papers.

The recommendations were accepted and the new examinations were introduced in 1951 with first candidates taking O-level papers in 1951 and A-level papers in 1953. In practice many of the intentions for the examinations at both O and A level proved impossible to achieve. The identification of purely 16+ target group and the linking of standards to the previous School Certificate were intended to restrict entry to mainly grammar school pupils following academic courses. However, headteachers' discretion determined the age of entry (at the suggestion of the Secondary School Examination Council) and unofficial board grading of results was eventually standardized and legitimated for both A-level (1961) and O-level papers (1975), with supplementary grading on S-level papers.

Nor were candidates drawn exclusively from academic streams and schools since entry was permitted in a limited range of subjects – indeed in even a single subject. S level also failed to play any important part in the allocation of university places. Indeed, as the numbers going on to higher education were increased in the 1960s, the proportion of candidates presenting S-level papers fell and A level came to be the major instrument of selection for higher education and a simple screening device for recruitment in other fields.

Given the interests of users, in particular the universities, it is not surprising that tensions exist between the school curriculum and the examination system. The educational content of courses leading to examinations is no longer entirely determined outside the schools and colleges but the potential for 'backwash' remains. The examination boards now seek to involve both providers and users, and teachers within the schools have the possibility of more direct influence upon the examinations and their syllabuses than would have been thought possible in the days of the School Certificate.

* Later these came to be called 'Special' (S-level) papers.

CONTROL OVER EXAMINATIONS

Although the influential role of examinations was quickly recognized, the position of the universities as the dominant providers was little disturbed by government intervention during the first half of this century. The GCE examinations continued this tradition which was substantially changed only through the development of the Certificate of Secondary Education in the 1960s.

Norwood had advocated that, in the interest of the individual child and of the increased freedom and responsibility of the teaching profession, control over the School Certificate examination should, over a seven-year period, pass to teachers. It was suggested that the School Certificate should be replaced by an internal examination conducted by teachers at the school on syllabuses and papers framed by themselves. Reform of the School Certificate, when it came, concentrated upon the introduction of the single-subject examination but left control largely in the hands of the university-based boards.

By comparison the introduction of the CSE examination brought about a massive increase in the number of teachers involved in examining. Unlike the slow tailoring of the GCE examination by traditional methods from the School Certificate, the creation of the CSE was rapid and original and it was drafted for a broader population. The new examination was offered in Mode III (a style of examining internal to a school or a small group of schools) as well as in Modes I (conventional external examining) and II (external examinations set upon the school's own syllabus). Because in some boards script marking was school-based with year to year standards guaranteed by board moderation of these marks, the examination increased the demands upon teachers' skills. Indeed, the training organized by the boards to meet these demands made a major contribution to teachers' knowledge and understanding of curriculum development and assessment techniques in general (Goacher, 1983b).

Research and development: evaluation and change

EXAMINATIONS AT 16+

Within two years of the introduction of the CSE examination a report was produced by the joint GCE/CSE Committee of the Schools Council* (Schools Council, 1966b) which stated: 'There are now two separate sys-

---

* At the inception of the CSE examination a joint GCE/CSE Committee had been established by the Secondary School Examinations Council and this was subsequently continued by the Schools Council.

tems of examining the attainments of pupils aged about 16. Yet the distribution of attainment is continuous ...'

The committee's terms of reference were to explore the relationship between the two examinations and to ensure that their organizations helped schools to choose between them solely on the educational needs of the pupils. While confirming that it had been wise to establish a link between GCE and CSE through the equivalence of grade 1, the committee questioned whether GCE candidates just failing to gain an O-level pass should receive no accreditation. As approximately 40 per cent of those entering the examination failed to pass, considerable numbers of candidates were (and are) involved. The almost inevitable conclusion was that:

... the national currency of results achieved by pupils who seek such a record [through GCE or CSE] seems to indicate that in the long run there will probably need to be a common certificate using a single descriptive system.

The committee recommended research and development work into the 'possibility of devising a method of describing results which would be common to both types of examination ... a common form of certificate'.

While suggesting that Mode III GCE examinations should be introduced on 'educational and practical grounds' and that approval for a new syllabus should therefore no longer be required,* the committee also stressed that the boards would need to review their arrangements

enabling teachers to play a major role in controlling the educational content of Ordinary level examinations.... The 'university' boards are conducting, as a service to schools and the community, an examination which has a dwindling role in the university entrance ... [It is not suggested, however] that the ... examinations should be under the exclusive control of teachers from participating schools. Higher and further education have a legitimate interest in courses of study which are specifically designed to lead naturally to the post-school courses for which they are responsible ...

In connection with the desired changes the committee pointed out that it was 'not recommending a revolution: there is no need for it'. It went on to advise against the introduction of graded O-level results, indicating that this could only be of value in predictive terms and that both the predictive validity and the reliability of the examination were low.

From such early considerations of the difficulties built into the examination system at 16 + the train of events had a certain inevitability. The way

* At this time a new GCE O-level syllabus required the endorsement of the appropriate subject committee of the Schools Council, previously that of the appropriate SSEC committee.

forward consisted of adapting to what was there and attempting to ensure the maintenance of a stable relationship between the twin examination systems. Radical reform, largely because it necessitated the replacement of the benchmark of the GCE, was, at least for a number of years, unthinkable.

The monitoring of the relationship between GCE O-level and CSE examinations has already been briefly referred to above. That piece of research was one of a series of exercises conducted by the NFER Examinations and Tests Unit (ETRU) over a twelve-year period. Although issues such as reliability, and validity and the uses of continuous assessment were explored, much of the Unit's work was focused on comparability at 16+.* Willmott (1980), summing up those years, pointed to a number of unresolved problems:

There is little doubt that the educational desirability of providing numerous syllabus options for pupils, teachers and schools has as its corollary first, that even with the most detailed scrutiny of the grading practices possible, some degree of 'incomparability' must exist and secondly, that whether or not comparability is achieved its existence cannot ever be verified completely ... If anything approaching strict comparability is to be achieved, and verified, then only a reduction in the number of syllabuses and in the wide variation of syllabus content organized by fewer examining boards will suffice ... The alternative to [this] strict comparability is a much more realistic approach to the use of the results from the examination systems which exist, or which may exist. The users of examination results should, perhaps, be told of the problems involved. But just how would this information be presented? It is not easy to see clear answers to such questions and any loss of confidence in the examination system could lead to a chaotic situation.

These issues emerge repeatedly in the account which will be provided of the use made of examinations and the views of users. They are central to the investigation although the balance between educational desirability, strict comparability and the realistic use of results remains delicate and unstable.

A report from the Joint GCE/CSE Committee, produced after their first eleven meetings (Schools Council, 1966b), proposed the development of a common grading system with the eventual objective of introducing common certification. By 1971 early reservations had been transformed into outline proposals for the development of a common system of examining at 16 + (Schools Council, 1971) and considerable research and development work to this end was undertaken.

The factors limiting the degree of comparability possible between

* Although ETRU no longer exists the work has continued. (See, for example, Johnson and Cohen, 1983.)

examinations, even when these carried the same title, were spelt out yet again by the Schools Council Forum on Comparability (Schools Council, 1979b). Three major factors were identified which limited the degree of precision which was attainable and which also contributed to inconclusive research findings. These were:

the nature of examination results in general;
the structure of the examination system in Britain; and
the nature of the grading schemes in the public examinations.

The reform needed to rationalize the dual system at 16 + appeared to receive official approval (DES, 1978b; DES, 1980b). However, redefined priorities following a change in the Secretary of State for Education and Science led in 1982 to a new policy document (DES, 1982b) which, while accepting the present unsatisfactory state of the examination system at 16 +, delayed the introduction of a new examination until such time as satisfactory national criteria could be agreed. The reasons given for change at that time included a number which were particularly pertinent to users:

CSE certificates have not been accepted;
the dual grading scheme confuses schools, pupils, parents and employers;
there are too many awarding bodies and too many syllabuses including an unnecessary number with the same title, and different titles which sometimes conceal only marginal differences in the scope of the syllabus;
the relationship between overlapping grades needs to be properly established.

EXAMINATIONS AT 17+

With increasing numbers of pupils remaining at school beyond a raised statutory leaving age and with many more of those having encountered the system of public examinations through CSE, it was not very long before a new examination population could be clearly identified. By the early 1970s this population of 'new', 'one-year' or 'non-traditional' sixth-formers had become the subject of much study and speculation. (See, for example, the NFER Alternatives to the Traditional Sixth Form Project, Vincent and Dean, 1977.)

Those remaining in school or going on to the new sixth form colleges were faced with only two alternatives – resitting 16 + examinations or entering the GCE Alternative O level (AO level). For those attending colleges of further education a range of broadly vocational courses offering group certification was a common alternative, and it was claimed by many that these courses were more likely to meet the needs of such youngsters than the AO papers which had initially been developed by the GCE boards to stimulate broader interests in the first year of those following traditional two-year A-level courses.

To meet the needs of such non-traditional sixth formers in schools a programme of extensive research and development was embarked upon by the CSE boards and the Schools Council from 1972. A pilot examination was conducted which, while it could not offer officially recognized certification, provided the evidence on which the Schools Council proposed the introduction of a new Certificate of Extended Education (CEE) in 1976. The government's Keohane Group (DES, 1979d) considered the proposal and after documenting the range of existing courses went on, in 1979, to support the introduction of a modified examination along CEE lines.

The CEE has remained experimental and relatively unknown outside educational circles, but has gathered many supporters within schools and sixth-form colleges. A parallel growth within the 16 + group in colleges of further education led to a plethora of new courses and the subsequent publication of the influential document *A Basis for Choice* (FEU, 1979).

The likely death knell of CEE was sounded with the publication of a new policy statement in 1982 (DES, 1982a). This document envisaged a system of courses leading to what was provisionally called the Certificate of Pre-Vocational Education (CPVE). The new 17 + examination was identified as 'broadly vocational' and 'unrelated to GCE or CSE examinations'. The statement pointed out that: 'The case for the new qualification rests on the unsuitability of GCE and CSE syllabuses as the basis for the pre-vocational courses which are needed for the target group.' The new CPVE will be a system of grouped courses administered by a Joint Board for Pre-Vocational Education established by the Business & Technical Education Council (BTEC) and City and Guilds of London Institute (CGLI), in the first instance based on existing one year pre-vocational qualifications.

EXAMINATIONS AT 18+

Not long after the introduction of GCE A level many of the same criticisms came to be levelled at the sixth-form courses which led to it, as had been made of those leading to the Higher School Certificate.

Some objections were related to what was seen as either the narrowness of the courses or the premature specialization to which even a three-subject

A-level course led. A series of alternative approaches were considered culminating in the formulation of proposals (Schools Council, 1978a and 1978b) for the introduction of a two-level examination (N & F).

Near the end of a lengthy exercise collecting together the reactions of all interested parties, these proposals were rejected by the then Secretary of State (DES, 1979c). However, the problems remained. The Schools Council was asked to make further recommendations (Schools Council, 1980b), and these (endorsed in outline in a DES consultative paper (DES, 1980b)) suggested broadening the sixth form curriculum by the development of a free-standing intermediate examination (I level) to be taken at 18+ alongside A levels. This examination was also seen as more appropriate to the needs of pupils at the lower end of the A-level range.

The nature of the curriculum leading to GCE A level, the examination itself and the implications for access to university have also been the subject of extensive study. Some of this work was conducted outside the framework of the Schools Council but most was conducted in response to Schools Council initiative or in collaborative ventures with other individuals or bodies.

The NFER study of transition from school to university (Choppin *et al.*, 1972) received some Schools Council funding. The research consisted of the development of an experimental Test of Academic Aptitude, its application and comparison with a range of other achievement measures and its eventual rejection as a suitable device in selecting for university places. S. Henrysson and I. Wedman (1979) came to a similar conclusion, finding that the predictive ability of meaned marks was rather better than that of the Swedish Scholastic Aptitude Test.

Studies by R. J. L. Murphy (1979 and 1980) explored the relationship between O- and A-level results and between teacher predictions and actual A-level results. Numerous studies have also been carried out to explore the relationship between A levels and degree performance (e.g. Bagg, 1968; King, 1973; Tinkler, 1978; Bligh, 1980; Wilson, 1980; and Rees, 1981). In general, those using small samples or single subjects found higher correlations than those using larger numbers on a broad spread of subjects. In one of the more recent studies, Rees (1981) concluded:

the A-level grades achieved by students were of little value in predicting degree performance ... The conditional A-level method of selection is simply an administrative convenience to obtain the target number of students rather than ... a scientific method of selecting those students most likely to obtain good degrees.

Other factors affecting admissions to higher education have also been the subject of research (e.g. Cohen, 1970; Reid, 1974).

Work in which the Schools Council has been directly involved includes studies of:

- entrance to Oxford and Cambridge (Lee, 1972);
- universities and the sixth-form curriculum (Reid, 1972);
- the examination courses of first-year sixth-formers (Schools Council, 1973b);
- paths to university (Hearnden, 1973); and
- a comparison of GCE A-level standards (Christie and Forrest, 1980).

Many of these themes re-emerged in the current study and form the core of Chapters II and III.

EXTENDING THE INFORMATION PROVIDED BY EXAMINATIONS

It is possible to provide a more detailed 'profile' of examination results. Present examining methods potentially offer information about more than mere accuracy of recall and, even within a subject discipline, distinct areas of knowledge and skill might be identified. Whether such information is wanted by users is more open to question.

Currently examination performance is presented to the user as a single grade, although individual paper, section and question scores are available to the examiner. It would be possible, as some boards already do, to include a separate score for practical papers in science and craft or for oral work in language subjects. Whether it is feasible or desirable to provide greater detail than this is still being explored both within examination boards and elsewhere. A. Harrison (1983), C. A. Newbold (1981) and K. Tattersall (1983) offer accounts of some of the problems and possibilities inherent in such approaches. User interest in alternative approaches to examination results is explored in Chapter IV.

ALTERNATIVES TO EXAMINATIONS

Criticism of examinations as indicators of ability and aptitude is not new and is documented in several of the publications noted above. The Norwood Report (Board of Education, 1943) specifically urged a greater dependence upon reports from schools and less reliance upon examinations. Recent years have, however, seen an increase in demands for evidence about aspects of individual performance, skill, interest and personal factors not readily provided by examinations. The development of profiles or records of achievement has been documented elsewhere (for example in Balogh, 1982; Goacher, 1983a; and DES, 1983) but the impact of this approach is still growing.

Many secondary schools have set about filling what they see as a gap in the system of certification and although some local authorities have co-ordinated the approach of their schools no more general scheme for providing an integrated record of achievement covering a much wider range of activity and performance has yet been put into practice. The Oxford Delegacy of Local Examinations, in collaboration with four LEAs, has declared its intention of developing a record to be validated by the board, and other boards have also begun work in this area.

An associated development is the boards' interest in graded tests where a series of test papers are designed to prove progressively more difficult; the intention is to enable candidates to progress as far as they are able. Such tests might be used to provide more reliable evidence for a profile. Many local authorities and some other examination boards are currently concerned in such developments. By contrast, others, including some groups of English teachers, have identified the graded test as an inappropriate tool in some areas of curriculum. On behalf of the Schools Council, A. Harrison (1982) has recently reviewed the use made of graded tests.

Users' attitudes to such alternatives to the information presently provided by examinations form part of Chapter IV.

EXAMINATIONS AND EMPLOYERS

By contrast with the wide range of activities which have been outlined so far, research concerned with exploring employers' use of, and attitude to, examinations is sparse indeed.

E. S. Freedman (1979) is one of the tiny band of authors who have worked in this field. Her work confirmed that many employers paid little heed to examination success (though some identified correlations between O-level success and subsequent performance), and that a majority were content with the educational standards of their recruits – a finding confirmed by E. Reid (1981).

D. N. Ashton and M. J. Maguire (1980), in a review of employers' selection strategies and the criteria used for recruitment, suggested that academic qualifications were not required for many vacancies and that 'many employers were ... cautious and circumspect in their use of ... certifications ...'.

The changing climate

It is not appropriate to give a lengthy analysis of social, economic, political and demographic change here. However, such factors are likely to have considerable influence upon the uses made of examinations and it would be equally inappropriate to ignore them.

The recent past has shown a continual steady increase in the annual numbers of young people reaching the statutory school-leaving age. This trend has now been reversed but the 1982/3 population of 18-year-olds is the largest the educational system has known. Concurrently the proportion of each succeeding cohort taking external examinations has also increased and there is no evidence to suggest that this trend will be rapidly reversed. However, many students still leave school uncertificated and some would suggest that many more are unqualified for the post-school world. It has been said that:

we have in the United Kingdom a history of persistent neglect of the majority of our young people once they leave school – a neglect that has been exposed in the light of increasing youth unemployment (FEU, 1982).

Users of examinations would have faced a problem of numbers in their selection processes in an era of economic stagnation. With economic decline the problem has been exacerbated.

In connection with previous work on school reports the author was made aware of an inflation in the demand for qualifications quite as dramatic as the fiscal inflation which was taking place. Those recruiting to technical apprenticeships in 1978, for example, felt that they could ask for applicants with three GCE O levels whereas three years earlier a similar number of average CSE passes would have been considered sufficient.

Economic difficulties have led to similar selection phenomena in the universities and this has been exacerbated as numbers have been influenced by central government through the University Grants Committee (UGC). Even if polytechnics are able to take up much of the overspill, as currently seems to be the case, the problem of efficiently screening out excessive numbers will remain for the universities. Evidence of a 'grade inflation' at the entrance to higher education similar to that described above will be documented in Chapter III, although the suggestion will also be made that some of the increase in barriers owes little to numbers and even less to course demands. Maintaining course status is also a factor.

In further education there has been growth which has more than matched the demographic trend. This can be identified as much as a function of the economic condition as of demographic change and it masks a quite dramatic change in the role of further education. As the numbers of sandwich course students have declined, overall numbers have been swollen by students on full-time courses who might, in other circumstances, have chosen employment. Central government funding, channelled through the Further Education Unit (FEU) of the Department of Education and Science, and more heavily through the Manpower Services Commission, had begun to have a considerable impact at the interface of full-time education and what follows it.

Expenditure in 1983 on 'youth training' reached one thousand million pounds and the numbers entering the Youth Training Scheme (YTS) exceed those going directly into employment. However, demand has proved difficult to gauge and teething problems have arisen. The influence of the MSC on the secondary curriculum has recently been extended through its Technical and Vocational Education Initiative.

An imbalance between skills and knowledge has been postulated and debate continues on the merit of moving to a skill-oriented course (see for example Duffy, 1983). While a case has been made that the position of the United Kingdom is unique in this respect, U. Teichler *et al.* (1980) have suggested that there are similar discussions taking place in many industrialized countries and that almost identical responses are discernible.

Within our own system the profile schemes used to document progress through and certificate the end-point of prevocational education and training are already indirectly influencing the educational sector and examinations. The market value of traditional qualifications may be affected, although whether examination certificates will lose or increase their value in occupational selection is, as yet, difficult to foresee. It was against such a background of intensive change and innovation that this study was carried out.

Methods

The time originally allocated for study was two years, although this was subsequently extended by three months to accommodate the disturbance caused by changes in personnel. Much of the information was necessarily collected by means of questionnaires, partly determining the type of questions which the Project could seek to answer.

To broaden the scope of the enquiry, discussions were held with the users of examinations wherever possible. The numbers of institutions involved in the study either through interview or questionnaire appear in Appendix A. Discussions were supplemented by the use of telephone interviews. It cannot be claimed that discussions of this type lead to conclusions which are statistically representative but they do offer valuable insights and a 'flavour' of the reality so often missing from a purely numerical study.

The sample

Within the school sector a stratified sample of users was obtained through Statistical Services at the National Foundation for Educational Research. In the areas of further and higher education a random sample of institutions was selected for inclusion. The final sample consisted of:

1 educational institutions using public examinations for selection at 16 +:
schools and sixth-form colleges
further education colleges (GCE and non-GCE courses)
non-degree courses in colleges of higher education and polytechnics
3 educational institutions using public examinations for selection and screening at 18 +:
degree and advanced courses in colleges of higher education
advanced courses in colleges of further education and polytechnics
degree courses in universities and polytechnics
3 employers using public examinations at 16 + and 18 + to assist with recruitment.

The information from this last sample was obtained through the work of Janet Jones, who was employed as BP Research Fellow at Reading University for a period of three years specifically to explore 'the use made by employers of public examinations and other tests'. Following a questionnaire survey of a stratified sample drawn from the Standard Industrial Classification (SIC)* in three geographical areas (South East England, West Midlands and Yorkshire/Humberside), she carried out a small number of case studies.†

The one-third sample of schools with sixth forms and sixth-form colleges was drawn to give a representative sample of comprehensive, grammar, independent and other schools (e.g. bilateral, technical) and sixth-form colleges in both metropolitan and non-metropolitan authorities from four regions (North, Midlands, South and Wales). Of the 1119 institutions identified, 29 were not used due to their present or recent involvement in Schools Council activities, 8 were excluded at the request of their local authority and 35 were incorrectly sampled (e.g. had no sixth form). The 784 questionnaires returned in time for analysis therefore represent a response rate of 75 per cent. A further 21 questionnaires were returned too late for inclusion.

The respondents included rather larger proportions of comprehensive

* 1980 revised edition.
† See also Jones (1983).

schools and grammar schools than might have been expected from the sample and a rather lower proportion of independent schools and sixth-form colleges. Details of the school sample appear in Appendix A, Tables 2 and 3. Where schools gave reasons for not taking part in the study these were most often concerned with staffing difficulties, recent or imminent reorganization or pressure of work.

The number of further and higher education colleges approached appears in Appendix A, Table 2. While no expectation of randomness can be assumed for the 234 college principals or the 351 tutors who were subsequently contacted in the area of further education and non-degree higher education, these contacts allowed access to a wide range of courses at all levels within further education. Although part-time courses were excluded from the study, those courses containing sandwich and block release students at the time of the survey were included.*

The number of colleges of higher education contributing to the study is shown in Appendix A, Table 2, together with the number of other institutions from higher education. The number of further and higher education courses studied is shown by level in Appendix A, Table 4; Tables 5 and 6 give details of all the courses included. Much of the non-response appeared to be due to sampled courses not running in the survey year.

The diversity of degree courses ensured that these too could only be sampled. Those studied were chosen to include courses where there was clearly the possibility of continuity with school subjects offered at A level (such as mathematics) and those where few candidates would be seeking to continue the same studies beyond A level (such as law). The complexity of the Oxford and Cambridge selection procedures and the subtle variations in role adopted by college admissions tutors prohibited the use of a postal questionnaire to come to a better understanding of the process. A semi-structured interview schedule was therefore used to explore the selection of candidates at a sample of Oxford and Cambridge colleges.

The views of the examination boards were also sought and many responded with written statements. A smaller number of boards were visited for discussion and visits were also made to the Standing Conference for University Entrance (SCUE) and the Universities Central Council on Admissions (UCCA).

---

* Apart from the separate treatment given to GCE A-level and degree courses the Department of Education and Science designation of courses (in DES, 1980a) was adopted.

Summary and matters arising

This chapter has described the origin of public examinations in Britain and has explored the way in which they have evolved.

A number of common themes were identified which link present provision to the past. Three of these major recurring issues were used to look at the developments of the past 126 years. Although views on these issues – the control of examinations, their impact on schools and the diversity of provision – have inevitably altered in response to changes in social climate, each has retained a central place in the debate.

While many observers continue to identify the universities as directly or indirectly responsible for the influence which examinations have acquired, university-based examination boards have sought to assure doubters of their autonomy, their freedom from university influence and their responsiveness to, and involvement of, secondary teachers. Nevertheless, some observers remain sceptical and point, for example, to the generally conservative influence that the university curriculum has had upon much of the work of schools. Chapter IV explores further the reactions of admission tutors in higher education to the board, syllabus and mode of examinations offered by applicants.

The role of central government in what Mitter (1979) has described as the 'free market system' of the United Kingdom, has largely been that of the arbitrator, seeking to moderate the excesses of the system without centralizing control. Whether such detachment will be maintained in the future is less certain.

While touched upon, the distinction between grouped and single-subject examinations was not explored in detail. Current developments at 17 + and MSC initiatives with the 14–18 age range may herald a return to grouped certification at a national level. Such a reassertion would have considerable implications for candidates and for users. The approach is explored further in Chapter V.

However, although diversity has largely been retained and even increased in terms of subject titles, recent years have also seen the growth of collaboration between the various providers of examinations. This trend has been maximized within the new structures established to facilitate the introduction of a common examination at 16 +. Such links will not readily be severed, although they may in time come to represent a new barrier to change.

Diversity, although providing the variety desired by many, has also given rise to contention over standards and this chapter has noted some of the attempts made to establish formal comparability. Comparability of a scientific and precise type is an almost impossible goal within such a devolved system, and Willmott (1977) has drawn attention to the importance that public confidence plays. It is for this reason that the perceptions of providers and users, described in Chapter IV, are of such crucial importance.

The use of public examination success to control entry to higher education was outlined together with emphasis on the failure of S-level papers to acquire any significant role in this process. Also noted was the lack of success of attempts to create a Test of Academic Aptitude, though whether any other mechanism could displace examinations from their central place in admissions to higher education is uncertain and, in the present climate, unlikely to be tested. Research into the comparative efficiency of meaned school marks as an alternative to public examination grades appears more promising although this is also an unlikely candidate for central funding.

The social context is not, however, static and this chapter has pointed to a number of changes which would undoubtedly affect the use made of examination results in the immediate future. In such a period of uncertainty it is hoped that this report will serve a useful function in documenting present practice and opinion and directing those who seek to improve the system along the most fruitful paths.

II. The use made of 16 + examinations

This chapter concentrates on the use made of the two major 16 + examinations, CSE and GCE O level. It collects the information provided by employers and by the whole range of institutions to which students may go.

Information from schools was normally provided by the head of sixth form, head of upper school, director of studies, deputy head or headteacher; that from sixth-form colleges by the principal, deputy principal or senior tutor. In colleges of further and higher education, however, the information was gained from tutors with responsibility for a single course.

The usual DES designation of 'advanced' and 'non-advanced' courses is used but, to aid comparisons between the school sector and further education, GCE courses – wherever provided – are considered together. To avoid unnecessary repetition sixth-form colleges will be included in the general description 'schools' except where they display different characteristics. Other non-advanced courses are described separately in this chapter and advanced courses are treated in Chapter III with other courses available at 18 +. The use made by employers of examinations at 16 + is explored in the penultimate section of this chapter.

Range of provision

The range of courses which can be supported by an institution partly depends on its size. Typically, school sixth forms contained 100 students (median), whereas the number found in sixth-form colleges was likely to be in excess of 400 and occasionally over 1000. There was considerable variation between the different types of school, with grammar schools (median sixth-form size 151) more likely to have large sixth forms than comprehensive schools (median 100). Interestingly, independent sixth forms were generally smaller (median 71) although, naturally, the constraints on provision are not necessarily the same as those within the maintained schools.

Schools wanting to extend their range of courses often formed consortia with other nearby institutions. This practice was found in over one-third of the comprehensive schools and almost one-fifth of the grammar schools, but in less than one in ten independent schools. Nine out of ten institutions offered post-16 GCE O-level courses while over one in three also provided CEE courses. The CEE was more frequently found in sixth-form colleges (eight in every ten) and comprehensive school sixth forms (almost half) than elsewhere.

Considerable differences were apparent in the range of A-level subjects offered by schools and in some cases these appeared to be related to the type of school. Almost one-third of the secondary modern school sixth forms did not offer an A-level mathematics course, for example, and this contrasted strongly with the figures of 1 per cent in other types of school. Certain other subjects were more frequently absent from the A-level curriculum in independent schools than that in the maintained sector. Physics, for example, was provided by only six in ten independent schools contrasted with eight in ten schools in the maintained sector.

GCE courses in the colleges of further education were sometimes distributed through most, if not all, departments but in almost one-third of the colleges such courses were concentrated into a general studies or liberal studies department. Responsibility for courses in about a quarter of the colleges was split between two of the larger departments, most usually science and humanities. Where a larger number of departments contributed to the organization of courses, timetabling and other matters of common interest were often taken over by a coordinator. It is interesting to note that departmental autonomy was one of the reasons given by further education colleges for being unable to accept a broadening of the curriculum as envisaged in the N & F proposals.

The larger size of further education colleges often allowed them to provide a broader spread of GCE courses. Thus A-level mathematics was offered in all but 4 per cent of the colleges and even the sampled subjects least likely to be represented, art, physics and French, were each available in nine out of ten colleges.

Overall, a quarter of the schools in the sample recorded that it had been necessary to limit the number of places on some courses due to a shortage of specialist space or equipment or because of insufficient qualified staff. Interestingly, this was rather more likely to happen in sixth-form colleges (over half), grammar schools (almost half) and independent schools (almost one third) than in comprehensive schools. Although this may relate to the size of school in the case of independent and grammar schools, it is difficult to suggest that this could be a convincing explanation in respect of sixth-form colleges.

The subjects affected were almost all sciences ranging from physics (creating problems in over a third of the schools) to chemistry (affected in almost one-fifth). Economics, mathematics and home economics were also mentioned but were referred to by less than a tenth of the schools reporting such difficulties. Rather more further education colleges recorded problems which limited the number of A-level students. In all, almost two-thirds of the colleges reported difficulties in some subject areas. Limited facilities were reported as affecting physics, chemistry, biology and psychology courses in many colleges.

These constraints were often seen as 'a justification for a more selective approach' (comprehensive school) and the effects were most likely to be felt by candidates coming from outside the institution. As one independent school put it, 'we ask for higher grades from external candidates'.

The question concerning the possible restriction of places evoked quite a different response from some quarters:

The opposite is occurring in this school – we are not able to run some A-level courses because of a lack of students and in fact many of our A-level classes are joint classes with upper and lower sixth together. (independent school)

The problem was duplicated in a number of further education colleges since in approximately one quarter of their courses there was also a shortfall of students. There were, however, distinct differences in the numbers of applicants to courses at different levels. For example, only 10 per cent of the A-level courses were over-subscribed whereas 40 per cent of other non-advanced courses received more applications than there were places.

A high level of demand for places occurred in over half the advanced courses included in the research, though the ratio of applicants to places varied widely between courses and colleges. Almost a quarter of advanced courses recorded four or more applications for every place. It was clear that while in some non-advanced and many advanced courses rigorous selection might be necessary to eliminate a large excess of applicants, this was not often true of GCE courses.

Although in the year of the study two-thirds of the courses received a greater number of applicants than in the previous year, few course tutors in further education considered that the level of qualifications offered by applicants had changed. Where tutors were aware of a change, for each individual who felt that the level of qualification had fallen, two considered that there had been 'noticable increase'. Such views, as will be shown later, contrasted quite dramatically with the more critical view of the achievements of school leavers expressed by employers. A number of college tutors also recorded a recent increase in the number of applicants seeking places at 17 + following a period of unemployment.

Sixth-form CSE courses were still offered in the majority of comprehensive schools and, rather more unexpectedly in the light of their subsequent views, were also available in over a fifth of the grammar schools and almost a quarter of the independent schools. Secretarial and commercial courses were rather more common in sixth forms of independent schools than in sixth-form colleges although in neither group were they offered by more than a quarter of institutions, whereas such courses were found in a majority of comprehensive school sixth forms.

City and Guilds (CGLI) courses were offered in less than 10 per cent of the maintained schools and in only a single independent school, but were found in almost half the sixth-form colleges. The courses available in colleges of further education could not be summarized in the same way and it was not possible to obtain any generalized picture of the alternatives open to a 16-year-old from such colleges. Even the relationship between the size of the institution and the range of courses provided was not open to easy interpretation since the proportion of part-time students fluctuated widely from college to college. The list of courses available nationally, provided in the *Directory of Further Education*,* extends to several thousand and the picture is further complicated by the variety of part-time and full-time modes of study as well as by course duration. Locke and Bloomfield (1982) offer the most comprehensive analysis of what they call 'the jungle' and make a series of suggestions to assist students through the maze of options.

While no institution offered more than a fraction of these courses, prospectuses suggested that many colleges were able to maintain a far greater flexibility than was apparent in the school sector, both in the range of courses offered and in the ability to include courses in the curriculum whenever student numbers allowed. Indeed the mechanism of student funding peculiar to further education appeared to be the factor most likely to limit student choice since it tended to restrict access to colleges other than those in the student's immediate locality.

Conditions applied to course entry

There are two possible major formal barriers to young people attempting to continue their education beyond the statutory leaving age. One comes at

---

* Published for the Careers Research and Advisory Centre by Hobsons Press, Cambridge.

the point of gaining access to the institution and the other at entry to a particular course of study.

The concept of open access to educational institutions is not one that has a long history in this country and, as the continued reaction to comprehensive schools adequately demonstrates, it is a principle that provokes a range of objections. Much has been written about the 'open access sixth form' but few of the institutions appeared to operate an open-to-all policy. Applicants almost always had to satisfy two sets of criteria, one connected with their previous academic performance and one to do with non-academic matters. Only through more detailed study than the Project was able to carry out could an accurate weighting for these two sets of criteria be determined. However, it was apparent that academic achievements were often used as a screening device, ensuring that all applicants with 'insufficient' academic credits were rejected. Non-academic criteria were then sometimes used to select from among those remaining.

Those seeking placement in courses provided by sixth-form colleges had come from a range of schools, both independent and maintained. The majority of sixth-form college students from the maintained sector were drawn from official 'feeder' schools although some were from maintained schools outside the designated catchment. School sixth forms tended to be home grown but almost one in ten had students from linked institutions. New recruits, however, seldom numbered more than a handful of students. Sixth forms in independent schools were most likely to be supplemented in this way although some sixth-form colleges also gained a significant proportion of their students from both nearby and distant independent schools.

The range of information received about new entrants varied only slightly between the different types of school and sixth-form college. The items most commonly included were teachers' predictions of public examination performance, assessments of the applicant's personal qualities and estimates of suitability for a sixth-form course. About one-third of the institutions were also given the official school record of most applicants. Over three-quarters of the course tutors in further education colleges received a similar range of assessments. Half also received the official school record.

As at all transitions within education, information provided by the previous institution was not always valued. Many of those receiving it pointed out limitations:

Some schools are very honest and if they recommend a student you do not really even need to interview. Other schools give minimal information ... some are very tight-lipped, they will not predict [grades], just say O level or CSE. We have also had some one-liners – '... has attended this school for five years' plus a signature – very damning. (college of further education)

Beauty, however, is in the eye of the beholder. The two following accounts were given by a sixth-form college and a college of further education situated in a fairly isolated market town and essentially drawing their population from the same feeder schools:

... we have a healthy contempt for what schools report to us, in fact we do not ask for reports because a break is a break. We don't trust reports; [they are] only the teacher's hasty, ill-informed comment without any degree of standardisation – very subjective and misleading. (sixth-form college)

... we generally get good references from [school] tutors so they are very useful ... Although some tutors lack knowledge of the world of further education, the reports are completed more accurately than ever before ... (college of further education)

The majority of independent and grammar schools had a formal academic barrier to entry whereas the proportion of comprehensive schools recording such a bar was only 16 per cent. Such barriers do not, of course, need to be formally erected and can be equally effective when they are created informally. Comments illustrating this approach included:

Theoretically we have an open sixth form but the courses we offer require at least CSE grade 3 for entry. In practice, no-one has asked to enter the sixth form whom we could not cater for. (comprehensive school)

Pupils who would not benefit are encouraged to find employment. (comprehensive school)

Formal exclusion policies may appear unnecessary in grammar schools and this was confirmed in a number of cases. While informal methods of exclusion might also be considered unnecessary there were indications that 'gentle persuasion' was employed, particularly in connection with the non-academic aspects of pupil performance. An example of this was given by a grammar school which had not 'actually refused' a place to any applicant:

... but there were one or two whom we were relieved not to have to teach because fortunately they left. In fact, the 'baddies' are usually not strongly motivated academically so [they] don't want to stay on ...

While such screening may also give rise to some transfers from independent to maintained schools not all independent schools demarcated so clearly between successful and unsuccessful students:

Your questions imply an old-fashioned policy of completing O level before commencing A level. If a pupil with a good record does badly at O level he may still go on to A level without a further year qualifying at O level to do so ...

Such sentiments were also discernible in some maintained schools:

The way these questions are phrased makes me feel our system is very informal. My main consideration is 'will this student benefit?' Some who enter the A level course 'without a chance' work very hard and mature in many ways over two years and sometimes even pass. Where we have 'failures' it is often with pupils who had a good set of O-level results. (comprehensive school)

While no information is available to indicate the proportion of applicants rejected by either formal or informal methods, and such detail would be almost impossible to document accurately, the response from schools suggested that the numbers involved were not large. However, one-third of schools had refused admission in the previous three years to individual applicants who were academically qualified for their chosen course and for whom a place would have otherwise been available. Rather more independent schools than maintained schools recorded that this had occurred. The major reasons given by schools for such an exclusion included 'poor attendance', 'disruptive' or 'anti-social' behaviour, a 'lack of motivation', a 'poor work record' and a 'lack of serious intention'. Sixth-form colleges added the withholding of a headteacher's recommendation from the applicant's school and rejection of out-of-catchment applicants due to a lack of places. One sixth-form college was prohibited from taking a mature applicant by the local authority.

Further education colleges often drew attention to the importance they attached to the concept of the 'fresh start'. A number pointed out that they would ignore accounts of poor performance or behaviour in an applicant's school career since they expected a more cooperative response in the 'adult atmosphere' of the college. Such students would only be asked to leave if new evidence of unacceptability emerged.

A number of tutors also spoke of the 'educationally bad' consequences of having to apply, rigidly, regulations demanding a specific number of O-level or CSE grades.

The attempt was often made to transfer rejected applicants to other less demanding courses and tutors drew attention to the eclectic nature of the provision within the further education sector. A few schools recorded their view that the 'fresh start' offered by some further education colleges could lead to students attempting courses for which they were unsuited and in which they were bound to fail.

The majority of schools interviewed all sixth-form applicants even when they were already following courses in the institution. This was less commonly done in the independent sector and over one-third of these schools did not interview applicants at all.

Because of the variety of courses available in further education and because of the wide differences in the academic demands made by these courses, the concept of a 'college barrier' appears inappropriate. Unlike schools, where individual subject demands are 'masked', admission procedures in colleges of further education take place at department level. It is, however, quite feasible in this area to obtain numerical information about the ratio of applicants to course places and this will be considered in the next section. Similarly, information concerning the interviewing of applicants was collected in connection with their application to courses, rather than to colleges.

Even within schools, traditional A-level courses can be analysed in a number of different ways. It is possible, for example, to consider them in terms of the overall demands they make, looking at them as one-, two- or three-subject courses. It is also possible to look in detail at the subjects and combinations of subjects involved. It is likely that a combination of these two approaches is used in most institutions. Appendix C provides an example of the course entry criteria developed by one institution.

ADMISSION TO A THREE-A-LEVEL COURSE

The full A-level course is usually considered to consist of three subjects chosen to offer a suitable basis for further study in higher education and possibly to meet specific career criteria. Schools were asked their 'normal minimum entry requirements' for a three-A-level course. The imposition of no formal academic criteria was rather more likely to occur in comprehensive schools than elsewhere although more than one in ten of all schools and almost one in ten sixth-form colleges said that they did not apply such restrictions. It is clear that the interpretation of this finding is subject to the same constraints that were outlined in connection with 'open' access at institutional level. The acquisition of five O levels (at grade C or better) or CSE grade 1 was the performance most commonly demanded. This academic criterion was applied in almost half the schools (seven out of ten independent schools) and in well over half the sixth-form colleges.

While the questionnaire suggested a 'normal minimum entry requirement' of five grade C O-levels or grade 1 CSEs a number of the independent schools indicated that their own minimum entry qualifications was more usually at six or seven O levels at grade C.

It was also clear that a small number of schools from both independent and maintained sectors specified O levels at grade A or B in some subjects. Such an approach was explicitly rejected by other schools:

No A-level subjects specify anything higher than a C at O level – it would be wicked to play safe and specify Bs. It would be malicious – the records show that C grades have proved quite adequate for a good A level. (maintained grammar school)

Most of the remaining schools and colleges set their entry standards to a three-A-level course a little lower, demanding four grade C O levels or grade 1 CSE passes. Less than one in ten schools and colleges had formal entry qualifications for a three-A-level course below this standard. The majority of traditional A-level courses in colleges of further education set their entry requirements a little lower than those demanded in the school sector. Well over half required four O levels at or above grade C or their equivalent. The common five-O-level school requirement was asked for by only 10 per cent of the further education college courses. GCE course tutors stating that they imposed no formal academic requirement for entry, were however only half as common as in the school sector, forming rather less than one in twenty of those in the survey.

In marked contrast to the procedures applied in the school sector, 40 per cent of GCE course tutors in further education colleges expected their applicants to take some sort of test. Most commonly this was a test devised in the college although one in ten included published test material. Less than one in ten tests involved the completion of an essay.

The major function claimed for testing was to establish basic competency in English and mathematics and thus to provide supplementary and diagnostic information which could be used to direct and aid students.

Course-specific tests were rare. In less than a quarter of the tests did 'failure' lead to an automatic rejection of the candidate and the pass mark was frequently varied in response to market forces. Such tests were seldom used to select students and the testing of all applicants was rare. The procedures were much more usually reserved for those whose qualifications fell short of those required for entrance or where objective information concerning an applicant's competency was not available. A few colleges tested only where there was uncertainty about the suitability of the applicant and some tested only those from overseas. One college of further education which made quite extensive use of its own tests explained:

The college tests for numeracy and literacy. We prefer to set our own test as few of us have confidence in the way in which mathematics is taught in many schools. Many people who should be all right struggle badly, the present maths qualifications don't mean they are numerate. A national test of numeracy and literacy might do. Our own tests are a multiple-choice paper for numeracy and a piece of prose in the form of a letter for literacy. We used to use NFER tests before devising our own but found they were not effective...

It was the normal practice in colleges of further education to interview all applicants. In the 14 per cent of cases where this was not so, applicants for interview were selected according to their predicted (marginal) examination results or if it was considered that they needed guidance in the selection of courses. Some colleges organized open days to meet this need.

The two most important matters which tutors explored in their interviews were the applicant's interest in the subject and their eventual career intention. These factors were both rated as 'very important' by more than half the tutors. Leisure interests and a student's likely contribution to the general life of the college were seen as unimportant by all but a minority but 'oral expression', the reasons given for seeking a college place and the applicant's 'temperament' were aspects pursued by a majority of interviewers. The 'temperament' aspects which were of most interest were work habits ('drive', 'willingness to work', 'self discipline' and 'motivation') and maturity ('reliability', 'reaction under stress', 'ability to work with others', 'adaptability'). A number also sought to discover if the applicant had parental support.

Almost half the tutors had refused admittance to suitably qualified candidates in the previous three years. Usually this had happened in response to a poor record from the candidate's school, particularly where this suggested criminal, violent or disruptive behaviour, poor motivation, behavioural problems or a poor record of attendance.

In contrast with the GCE courses in the school sector, over 90 per cent of the courses in further education included 'mature' students over the age of 21. In a very few cases such students comprised a third or more of the students on the course although typically they formed less than one in ten of the course numbers.

ADMISSION TO A TWO-A-LEVEL COURSE

For two-subject courses a number of institutions in the school sector insisted upon the same level of examination performance as that demanded from a three-A-level applicant although such schools did not form quite ten per cent of the total. In colleges of further education such a condition was set by only one in twenty of the courses and no sixth-form colleges erected such a high hurdle to applicants. Such barriers were most firmly asserted in the independent schools, where almost a quarter applied such a restriction, and in grammar schools where the proportion exceeded one in ten.

Most commonly the entry requirement for such a course was set at four grade C O levels or their equivalent. This was demanded by more than four in ten of the schools, by rather more of the sixth-form colleges and by half of the further education colleges. Three grade C O levels were expected by most of the remainder of the schools and colleges although rather more claimed that they had no formal academic entry requirements for the two-A-level course than had done so for the traditional programme. Almost one in twenty of the courses in further education colleges also claimed this. Perhaps unsurprisingly, quite large proportions of the independent schools (15 per cent) and the grammar schools (17 per cent) indicated that they did not offer such courses. It was not possible to determine whether this reflected a concern for academic respectability, a rejection of programmes of uncertain market value, or a decision not to provide for all needs.

ADMISSION TO A SINGLE-A-LEVEL COURSE

In the light of the above finding it was quite predictable that almost half the independent schools and grammar schools would not allow students to take a course offering a single A level; nor was it possible to follow a single-A-level course in almost a third of the colleges of further education. In most of the remaining schools (over two-thirds of the comprehensive schools) a student would only be allowed to study a single A-level subject 'in exceptional circumstances'. This position was almost exactly duplicated in sixth-form colleges and in colleges of further education. Where single A levels were taken, they were often integrated into a 'package' of commercial or technical subjects certificated in some other way and the subjects involved reflected this orientation. Those occurring most frequently among the single A levels studied in schools were art, design and technology, craft and needlework. In colleges of further education, subjects most frequently studied in isolation also included art but thereafter showed considerable differences. The subjects ranged from basics such as English language and mathematics to science (biology) and the social sciences (sociology, government and politics).

SUBJECT VARIATION IN CONDITIONS OF ADMISSION

The requirements demanded for entry to a number of named courses were also explored in some detail.* In general they reflected the marked change

* The subjects studied were art, biology, economics, English literature, French, history, mathematics and physics.

in the link between GCE examinations at O and A levels which has taken place since these examinations were introduced. At their inception, it must be remembered, they were seen, in the context of individual subjects, to be almost mutually exclusive. If a subject was to be pursued at A level it was intended that it should not be taken at O level.

The original description indicated that A-level certification would confirm that O-level requirements had also been satisfactorily completed. An O-level grading was included at the bottom of the 'acceptable' scale of A-level performance to allow for this to be indicated where performance of the candidate warranted this alone. That, of course, ignored the reality of the need to follow a pre-16 course for many subjects if they were to be taken thereafter. Once a course was being followed there was the usual social pressure to validate and certificate the result.

Subject entry requirements which demand proof of an existing competence in the same subject can also be seen as a reflection of commonly held views concerning the sequential nature of the material in some disciplines. Similar opinions are widely held about the difficulty of some subjects and the time students require in order to master them. It was perhaps to be expected, therefore, that 95 per cent of all institutions demanded mathematics at O-level grades B or C before allowing applicants onto a mathematics A-level course. In the case of courses in physics and French similar demands were made in 90 per cent of institutions, although in grammar schools the picture was identical to that described for mathematics. For other subjects, the proportion of schools demanding at least a B or C grade at O level in the same subject was smaller, with the proportion seeking such conditions being, for example, three-quarters in biology, two-thirds in English literature and three-fifths in history and art.

Throughout the whole range of subjects looked at in detail the entry conditions imposed by independent schools were in general higher than those in the maintained sector. Thus 75 per cent of independent schools required proof at O level for entry to an English literature course; for history the proportion was 68 per cent.

In colleges of further education, although the pattern remained essentially the same as that in the school sector, rather fewer institutions made such specifications. Thus, two-thirds of the colleges required an O-level grade B or C in biology, four out of ten colleges in English literature and just over a third in history. The exception to this general rule appeared to occur in the case of art, where considerably more than two-thirds of colleges required at least an O level grade C.

Some A-level subjects do not have a commonly taken O-level equivalent; this situation arises again at the boundary between A level and degree course (see Chapter III). In the case of economics, for example, almost two-thirds of the schools and sixth-form colleges made no further academic demands beyond those related to general entry to the sixth form. One-fifth of the schools, however, still recorded that they would expect at least a B or C grade at O level in a 'related' subject before accepting a student on an A-level economics course.

THE EQUIVALENCE OF CSE GRADE 1

Since CSE grade 1 is defined as equivalent to an O-level grade C or above, it should present few problems of acceptability as an entrance qualification, particularly to schools. Nevertheless the acceptability of a CSE grade 1 in certain subjects was explored for a range of courses.

In approximately one-quarter of the grammar schools and half of the independent schools the question hardly arose, since CSE courses were not taught or candidates who followed CSE courses did not attempt to enter the sixth forms. However, in other institutions the acceptance of CSE grade 1 as an O-level equivalent almost exactly mirrored the pattern already described in respect of specific subject requirements at O level. Thus, where CSE was available as an alternative in the subject concerned, it was rejected by almost a third of the schools as a suitable qualifying examination for A-level mathematics and by a quarter of the schools as giving entrance to A-level courses in physics and French. Between a quarter and a third of all schools and colleges would allow candidates offering a CSE grade 1 to enter a group working towards an A level in mathematics, physics and French but did not recommend this course of action. The proportion of schools and sixth-form colleges indicating that they were happy to allow applicants with CSE grade 1 to enter such a group was, for physics, mathematics and French, little more than one in ten. In those grammar schools and independent schools where CSE in these subjects was taken, the proportion refusing to accept it approached 50 per cent.

Where the subject was English literature, history or biology, the proportion of schools not allowing applicants with CSE grade 1 into an A-level course was near to one in ten and those 'happy' to accept such applicants approached a third of all schools and colleges. In these subject areas between a quarter and a third of the independent schools still refused places to such applicants. In the case of biology, over one in five of the grammar schools followed a similar course of action. Approximately one-fifth of all schools and colleges, while accepting biology, history and English literature applicants with CSE grade 1, still advised against their entry. Only in respect of applicants to A-level art courses did the proportion of schools and colleges rejecting candidates with CSE grade 1 fall to one in twenty and those happy to accept it rise to over half the sample.

Schools justified or rationalized their actions in a number of ways. While some stated baldly that the two qualifications were just not equivalent, others indicated that for some subjects the method of working adopted in the CSE course was not an appropriate training for the A-level course. Others indicated that the subject matter covered in the CSE syllabus failed to provide a sufficient grounding for the A level to be followed without great difficulty. Some teachers with lengthy experience in teaching their subjects across the full secondary age range made their opinions quite clear:

In my subject a large number do CSE and many end up with a grade 1 but they are still not capable of O level ... the syllabus is not as far reaching. Although I tell people with grade 1 that it is equivalent it really is not. As you go down through the CSE grades it gets worse ... grade 4 as a norm ... nobody takes that seriously ... to get grade 5 is really a condemnation not a certification ... (head of mathematics, mixed comprehensive school)

Others suggested that:

O level ... tests real things – mental ability, memory – though not necessarily real subjects ... it takes the population concerned and finds out which young people have attained a certain degree of mental development. CSE does not test these things at all ... it tests conformity, a very basic degree of educational attainment plus hard work, regularity, etc. (sixth form tutor, mixed comprehensive school)

The two extremes in terms of subject differences were captured by comments such as:

CSE grade 1 in language is a particular problem due to the nature of the syllabus. CSE is not an adequate preparation for A level. (senior tutor, sixth-form college)

and

CSE grade 1 is more than adequate for Design A level – probably better than O level. (sixth form tutor, mixed comprehensive school)

Because the target population for CSE extends well beyond that of GCE O level the examination has essentially different aims. The syllabuses are distinctive as are the tasks set for candidates. Equivalence exists in terms of the overlap in ability between the two sets of candidates and not in terms of their experiences and knowledge. The headteacher of a mixed grammar school spelled out the dilemma this causes for many admissions tutors:

Neither CSE or O level are terribly good predictors of A level performance; even an A or B at O level does not necessarily mean that a student will do well. I find this applies especially in mathematical subjects. In the sciences, CSE people have terrible trouble. This is not their fault but is related to the syllabus content and to the method and style of teaching ... we do accept CSE grade 1 as equivalent to O level ... but people with CSE physics have found it very difficult and there hasn't been a single success with CSE mathematics and A level.

While the acceptability of CSE examinations in general was not followed up in such detail in colleges of further education, it was expected that the colleges would receive many applications from holders of CSE certificates and the matter was pursued for a range of subjects. The subject pattern which has now emerged on a number of occasions was repeated once again. A-level courses in mathematics, physics and French were those which most commonly recorded that they would not allow entry to candidates offering a grade 1 CSE in the same subject. The proportion of mathematics courses where this occurred was more than a fifth and in less than one in ten were tutors 'happy' to allow entry to such candidates. In other subject areas an outright refusal was rare and the proportion advising against entering an A-level course fell below one in ten in art. Similarly, it was only in art that a majority of tutors would be happy with such candidates, although almost half of the tutors in history and economics recorded the same view. Elsewhere the majority of tutors would allow entry but considered that such candidates would be likely to have problems with the course.

Tutors in colleges of further education recorded another aspect of equivalence, that of recognition by employers. Some pointed to the need for a 'massive public relations exercise' and their own attempts to change the 'intractable', 'parochial' and 'dreadful' attitude of local employers who 'completely discounted' the value of CSE even at grade 1. In the light of the preceding paragraphs it might be thought that the education sector is also in need of a similar exercise to change ingrained attitudes.

THE EFFECTS OF SYLLABUS DIFFERENCES ON ADMISSIONS PROCEDURE
Similar reasons were given by schools and colleges for the practice of discriminating against a particular syllabus, although in this case no distinction was apparent between GCE and CSE examinations. The proportion of institutions discriminating on the basis of syllabus was much smaller than that rejecting the equivalence of CSE grade 1; overall it only represented 6 per cent of the sample. Once again such patterns of selection were more common in sixth-form colleges, grammar schools (one in five)

and the independent sector than they were in comprehensive schools. The incompatibility of their own courses with syllabuses pursued elsewhere provides one possible explanation for such actions in sixth-form colleges, but cannot explain their incidence in grammar and independent schools where there are fewer outside applicants.

Mathematics and science were the subject areas most often identified as presenting problems, although many schools indicated that they would treat each case individually. Conversions from SMP (School Mathematics Project) to 'traditional' mathematics and vice versa were seen as most problematic.

The 'adjustment' of applicants' grades to take account of the syllabus which they had followed was rather more commonly practised in colleges of further education than in the school sector, being reported by about one in ten of the colleges involved. Interestingly, the same number claimed to make similar adjustments in connection with examination modes. Comments by respondents drew particular attention to Mode III examinations* in this respect. It is difficult not to view such practices with an element of irony in the light of the continued attempts over many years to increase the element of teacher involvement in public examinations. Torrance (1982) has also pointed out that Mode III examinations present an ideal opportunity to tailor a public examination to subsequent needs.

Only 3 per cent of the questionnaires confirmed that such adjustments were made for the examinations provided by particular GCE and CSE examining boards. Additional comments suggested that some teachers were concerned with what they perceived as differences in standard between examinations offered in the same subjects by different examination boards, whereas others identified different subjects examined by the same board. A representative comment dealing with the first aspect reported:

I have taught [Board A's] O-level mathematics in my previous school ... it was much more difficult that the [Board B] syllabus I currently teach ... I would like to see some standardization of the boards. ... (sixth form tutor, boys grammar school)

An example of the subject differences was provided by a sixth-form tutor in a comprehensive school:

The standard of difficulty is not parallel even between subjects within the same board. It is, for example, 'too easy' to pass English language and 'too difficult' to pass German and physics.

---

*The syllabus and papers of a Mode III examination are designed within a single school or a group of schools. Both syllabus and examination are, however, checked by the board and the subsequent grades are awarded after scrutiny.

THE POSITION OF APPLICANTS WHO HAVE FAILED TO GAIN AN O LEVEL

Schools and colleges of further education were asked about their attitudes towards applicants who failed to obtain O level, or its equivalent, in a subject they intended to pursue. In light of the barriers to admittance which have been documented so far it was surprising to find that few institutions identified this as a problem area.

Perhaps this is because students do not press their case, or perhaps it reflects the attempt by most institutions, even where they are dealing with large numbers of applicants, to consider the case of each candidate individually.

In the school sector only 4 per cent claimed that they would not allow access to an A-level course when the candidate had failed to obtain an O level. There was a marked contrast in this respect with the further education sector, where almost a quarter of the colleges were not prepared to allow students to start an A-level course in a subject where they had previously failed at O level. One quarter of all schools claimed that the giving of such permission was not uncommon, a view confirmed in only one in twenty of the further education colleges, while the majority (seven in ten schools and more than five in ten colleges) described the giving of places to such applicants as only being permitted in 'exceptional circumstances'.

Here, as in so many other respects, there were quite marked differences between the different types of school. Comprehensive schools were the least likely to reject such applicants, with only 2 per cent recording this attitude, whereas candidates failing O level in the subject they intended to pursue in the sixth form were three times more likely to be rejected by grammar schools and sixth-form colleges, and the proportion of independent schools recording rejection was five times as large.

The effect of O-level failure was explored in greater detail in two subject areas, English literature and mathematics. The pattern in both subjects was remarkable for its uniformity across the whole range of institutions. As might have been expected from previous descriptions there were, however, distinct differences between the subjects. Rather less than one in ten schools recorded the presence of first-year mathematics students who had not met the entry conditions. In further education colleges the proportion was slightly higher but remained close to 10 per cent. In English literature one-fifth of the schools recorded the presence of such students in their lower sixth-form groups. Once again courses in further education were rather more likely to contain such students and they were recorded in almost one-third of the English literature courses in this sector.

While such variation can be explained in terms of perceived subject differences, the questions which prompted the responses were framed to explore the extent to which discretion was exercised by those admitting sixth-form students. It was clear that, although institutional rules are frequently blamed by teachers and others for imposing inflexibility, much more of the variation was caused in this case by the conceptual strait-jacket of subject perceptions and by variations in the criteria which were associated with the different subject disciplines.

Some explanations offered for the relaxation of the entry criteria could clearly not explain the dramatic subject differences. It is improbable, for example, that 'changes of teacher', 'illness' and 'family difficulties', which were offered as reasons for poor examination performance, would correlate more highly with English literature than with mathematics. These types of problems may, of course, receive greater attention from teachers of English literature than from teachers of mathematics. Other explanations given could be seen as having possible subject correlations. The relative ease with which it is considered possible to examine accurately in mathematics is one such factor. Thus 'unexpected' and 'inexplicable' examination results were more common in English literature than in mathematics and many respondents felt that English O-level results in both language and literature were particularly unpredictable.

A further factor, also related to essential differences in the perceptions of the two subjects, concerned the purpose of following an A-level course. A number of schools agreed with the proposition that '... English is a subject where girls can gain much from just following the course' (independent girls' school), and some would certainly consider that boys too could benefit. It was also apparent that English language was considered as acceptable preparation for a literature course. In some schools, of course, English literature was not offered at O level.

POST-16 O-LEVEL COURSES

Over 90 per cent of schools included one-year O-level courses in their sixth-form curriculum. It was the most common provision after A level. Similarly only 6 per cent of the respondents from further education recorded no O-level provision. Such one-year courses were least likely to be included in the range of courses offered by grammar and independent schools although even there they were absent from only one in seven schools. One grammar school explained its policy as one of allowing O level to be retaken 'only if the subject is strictly necessary ... otherwise it is felt to be too great an interference with the A-level course'.

In general, courses were open to O-level candidates even where their previous performance had been ungraded, although up to a third of the institutions including courses required that the previous performance had been graded at D or E. Sixth-form colleges and comprehensive schools were rather less likely to apply this restriction than other schools. In a majority of the one-year O-level courses offered in colleges of further education candidates were accepted even where their first attempt had produced an ungraded result. Only in physics and French did the majority insist upon a previous D or E grading but the situation was fairly evenly balanced in mathematics, history and biology.

There were minor differences between the subjects on offer in schools but most of this appeared to be due to the varying availability of resources. Rather less facilities were available to retake O level in science subjects ('repeat' physics and biology courses were not available, for example, in a quarter of the schools) than in 'arts' courses such as English language and history, both of which were available in 95 per cent of the institutions. Some sixth-form provision may, of course, consist of joining a fifth-year group and this would, because of practical work in the sciences, prove more feasible in the case of arts courses.

Where the possibility of resitting an unsuccessful O-level subject in the autumn term was offered, most schools and sixth-form colleges were inclined to demand a D grade at the previous performance or, exceptionally, grade E.

Candidates were commonly allowed only a limited number of 'repeat' O levels – usually two or three – whether they were to be attempted in the autumn or after a full year's course. A number of schools also recorded that in some areas students were expected to meet the repeat examination fees which were subsequently refunded where candidates were successful. These references to a 'double penalty' hinted at an interesting area of enquiry, but no formal investigation of fee-paying practice was possible. One part of double-entry fees at 16 + (GCE and CSE in the same subject) is not uncommonly paid for by parents. Current economies in educational funding may lead more schools and authorities to pursue this practice despite the obvious risks of inequity.

Not all students following a one-year O-level course were resitting the examination. Some were attempting to 'convert' a CSE certificate into an O level. The very existence of such students offered further confirmation of the difference in value placed upon the GCE and CSE examinations although almost half of the institutions recorded that this situation did not arise.

Where former CSE students were allowed to attempt 'conversion', a previous performance at or above grade 3 in the same subject appeared to represent the critical threshold. Although the provision of courses varied considerably according to the subject, in each case 80 per cent or more of schools demanded a grade 3 or better before allowing access. This held true over a wide range of subjects including English language and mathematics – in which many schools offered appropriate courses – and physics and French, where far fewer opportunities were available to applicants.

CSE/GCE 'conversion' students were a relatively unknown phenomenon in the grammar and independent schools and many sixth-form colleges pointed out that they did not offer this provision as they had the resources to offer suitable alternative courses, most commonly CEE. A number of schools and colleges of further education reported their dissatisfaction with a system which in their experience produced 'quite a high failure rate for the conversion from CSE and with O-level repeats'.

THE EXISTENCE OF 16+ 'CORE'

The extent to which sixth forms attempted to ensure that all students secured a 'satisfactory qualification' in English and mathematics was explored in an unstructured way.

Although two-thirds of the schools and rather more of the sixth-form colleges and colleges of further education claimed that they had a policy, this usually consisted of 'encouraging' rather than enforcing student compliance. This should not be seen as necessarily diminishing its effectiveness for, as one teacher noted, 'no-one has so far ignored my advice'! In some cases it was the curriculum content which was prescribed rather than a specific examination and, even where examination success was the ultimate objective of the policy, it was clear that this did not have to be in GCE O level. The range of examination courses, especially within sixth-form colleges, was quite wide and included CEE and Royal Society of Arts (RSA) and less commonly CGLI and BTEC alternatives.

There was, however, a small group of schools which insisted that all traditional three-A-level candidates should obtain O levels in English and mathematics. In a minority of colleges of further education both mathematics (or arithmetic) and English examination courses were insisted on for students without such qualifications, although in almost as many colleges an English course alone was mandatory. Once again the range of courses on offer included RSA and CGLI qualifications. One college of further education where O-level English language was 'compulsory' recorded:

Anyone who comes without O-level English language will go on taking it until they get it. The record is nine sittings – someone who went on to get a first and then a Ph.D. at Imperial College.

Full-time non-advanced courses other than GCE

The way in which selection was carried out for non-advanced courses other than GCE is considered separately for two reasons: such courses were relatively uncommon in the school sector and many applicants to courses had a markedly different educational history from that which characterized applicants to traditional A-level courses.

The range of courses available has been considered earlier, when it was made clear that the potential competition for places on these courses was high in only a minority of cases (in four in ten courses). Although some comments suggested that the shortfall of candidates for such courses was a fairly recent phenomenon, only one in ten recorded that the number of applicants had fallen in comparison with the previous year. Such courses typically provided places for rather more than thirty students. A list of courses included appears at Appendix A, Table 5.

Tutors confirmed that, as with GCE candidates. the level of qualifications offered by those applying to other non-advanced courses had been maintained in the current year. While the size of the majority holding this view was similar (over two-thirds of those questioned), a rather higher proportion said they considered that there had been a noticeable increase in the level. This opinion was recorded by a quarter of the tutors of non-advanced courses.

Rather more than half of the non-advanced courses contained no mature students. When present they seldom formed more than one in ten of the current students. In the admission procedures for such students, colleges were often able to waive the formal academic requirements and to place a greater emphasis upon experience or an employer's reference.

Teacher predictions of examination performance, assessments of suitability for the course and of personal qualities were available in almost all cases to help with selection. Interestingly, school records were rather more commonly made available than had been the case with applicants for more traditional post-16 courses. Well over two-thirds of the tutors claimed that they received the official school record of those coming to courses straight from school.

Ninety per cent of the tutors interviewed all applicants. Where this was not so, late applicants, those who had previously passed a test of some sort, 'mature' and 'marginal' applicants were those most usually focused upon. Interview criteria were similar to those already discussed in relation to application to GCE courses, in that most interviewers agreed on the importance of determining the candidate's interest in the subject and career intentions but paid little attention to leisure interests or likely contribution to the college life. Those interviewing for other non-advanced courses placed less importance upon oral expression and temperament than had the GCE interviewers. Where particular aspects of temperament were identified they were usually framed in terms of the applicant's 'willingness to work' 'adaptability' or 'pleasantness'.

College tutors were asked about the relative importance of their own selection criteria and those prescribed externally. In the area of non-advanced courses diverse opinions were expressed. Some suggested that in such adverse market conditions, colleges were compelled to accept 'whatever employers dictated'. Elsewhere, college rigidity in applying academic entry requirements was seen as inappropriate and was condemned.

The range of procedures adopted for non-advanced courses available in a single college of further education was illustrated by one tutor:

For Business Studies the constraints are largely those of the professional bodies. For BEC National a four O-level cut off is strictly applied – for BEC General three to five CSEs. There is also a pre-entry test for Business Studies and for BEC General and the Secretarial Diploma. All those who pass are offered a place on at least a low level course – BEC General or an Office Studies course leading to RSA qualifications. Those not recruited are channelled to other departments, sent back for counselling or told to take their chance in the world of work ... For City and Guilds Catering academic criteria are not very important – entry is largely based upon the subjective view of the Head of Department although this is backed up to some extent by references and the predicted CSE/O level attainment – the standard of English needs to be reasonable ... For the Hotel Reception course the correlation between the success rate and O level is fairly high ... Agricultural Mechanics is not tied to sixteen plus achievement for the pre-Diploma course, since the main aim is to get students up to OND level, two or three O levels are required ... General Art and Design – four O levels are required ...Engineering construction has a four O level entry but is very flexible ... Most departments are fairly traditional and see CSE or O level as valuable selection criteria ... It used to be unpolitic to turn people away from the A-level course with CSE but now people are tending to say ... they may not be able to cope ... CSE [grade] four and five are diagnostically meaningless for some courses but for something like BEC General or Introductory Engineering they do have some usefulness.

It was clear from the returns made by full-time course tutors* that opinions concerning the relative importance of internal and external

* Courses for 'block release' or 'sandwich course' students currently involved in at least one year's full-time study were included.

criteria were almost evenly divided, with approximately half recording that the entry requirements were determined by college staff. Where the entry requirements were determined by outside bodies these were more likely to be 'followed closely' than 'rigidly adhered to'. In almost 10 per cent of the courses tutors reported that such entry requirements were 'modified' to suit the particular circumstances in which they worked.

Where applicants were under the age of 21, over three-quarters of the courses stipulated an entry requirement which included evidence of some public examination success. The lowest such requirement was framed in terms of having followed a CSE course at school without demanding specific grades at examination. Almost one in ten of the non-advanced courses set their entry at this level. CSE grade 4 was of particular interest since this theoretically represented a 'national average' achievement. Entry was set at the level of three or four CSE grade 4s by 3 per cent of courses indicating that very few non-advanced courses were open to those at, or below, the national average of achievement as measured by CSE. The largest single group of courses, representing almost four in ten, had entry requirements set at the level of four O levels Grade A, B or C or the same number of passes at CSE grade 1. One in twenty of the courses had more stringent requirements than this. CSE grade 1 was accepted almost universally as equivalent to at least grade C at O level for these purposes.

Where entry requirements included a named subject this was most likely to be English (asked for by almost half the courses), mathematics (required by just under a quarter of courses) or 'science or mathematics' (stipulated for over a fifth of the courses). Subjects which were identified as 'desirable but not essential' showed exactly the same order of priorities but did indicate that a small number of courses showed a preference for practical and technical subjects or subjects related specifically to the course in question.

Considerable variation was apparent in the level of qualification demanded by tutors selecting candidates for identical courses in different colleges. While one might expect some variety in the entry qualifications required for college-based courses, and this was apparent, such variety was also found among those courses validated by national bodies. Examples of this included courses validated by the London Chamber of Commerce (e.g. Private Secretary's Certificate, where entry requirements ranged from 'two O levels at grades A, B or C' to 'five GCE passes including one at A level'); the Technical Education Council (e.g. TEC Diploma in Civil Engineering Studies, with a range from 'three to four grade 4 CSE passes' to 'four O-level passes at grades A, B or C'); the Business Education

Council (e.g. BEC General Diploma in Business Studies, where requirements ranged from 'should have followed a CSE course but no grades specified' to 'four O levels at grades A, B or C'); and the City and Guilds of London Institute (e.g. CGLI Ladies Hairdressing Certificate, with a range from 'should have followed a CSE course although no grades specified' to 'three O levels at grades A, B or C'). Such widely differing levels of entry qualification for what are clearly courses with a national currency, while no doubt accurately reflecting local variation in the demand for particular qualifications, raise doubts about the equity of provision. When the barrier to student choice imposed by the local base of student grants is taken into account such variation must result in personal injustice as well as a waste of national talent.

The acceptability of qualifications other than O level and CSE was explored although it must be remembered that such qualifications are unlikely to be held by many other than mature applicants. Perhaps for this reason the questions were usually answered by a minority of respondents, typically less than one in five of those questioned. With such limited information it is difficult to assess the general acceptability of alternative qualifications. However within this small group of tutors BEC, TEC, OND, ONC and CGLI qualifications were declared acceptable by a ratio of two tutors to one, and RSA certificates were accepted by half of the tutors. CEE qualifications were described as acceptable alternatives by a few tutors and a number also included 'overseas O-level equivalent qualifications'.

The number of tutors claiming that they 'adjusted' the grades required of candidates, to take account of the syllabus examined, the GCE or CSE board concerned or the mode of examining, was tiny and could not be considered to have any effect upon the general pattern of admissions.

Tutors were asked to estimate the nature of the lowest, average and highest qualifications held by current students. Very few tutors identified students without formal academic qualifications. When the position was looked at across the full range of non-advanced courses it was clear that a typical student at the 'lowest' level would hold a range of CSE passes, mainly at grades 2 or 3, a typical student in the 'average' position would have three O levels at grades A, B or C, or CSEs at grade 1, and a typical student from the 'highest' range would have gained five O levels at grades A, B or C or their equivalent.

Further evidence was therefore offered in support of the view already expressed that there were few opportunities for students with evidence of a level of achievement at about the national average as recorded by public examination. It did, however, appear that the 'typical' student with an average number of qualifications had performed at rather below the level most often set for entry to non-advanced courses (i.e. four O levels at A, B or C or their equivalent). A further question clarified this matter and confirmed that almost four out of ten of the current students had not reached the 'minimum' entry requirement for the course where this included public examination results. This phenomenon should perhaps be construed in terms of the pressure to maintain a full course since it cannot be accounted for by, for example, the proportion of applicants receiving unconditional offers of places prior to their results being available. Typically such unconditional offers were made to less than 20 per cent of the applicants.

Entry to higher education

A number of admissions tutors in polytechnics and universities and those selecting students for advanced courses in colleges of further education drew attention to the importance they attached to 16+ qualifications. Many identified them as the most important piece of evidence concerning a candidate's achievement available at the time of selection. Thus one polytechnic tutor gave the priority for initial selection from application forms as:

1 O-level results to date (points for grades)
2 Educational reference
3 The interests of applicants
4 Predicted A-level grades

More commonly tutors saw O-level grades as of secondary importance to predictions of grades at A level.

16+ qualifications were often seen as providing evidence of the 'breadth' of a candidate's experience which was missing from the information provided by A level. Not all tutors saw the value of O level in such clear-cut terms. One polytechnic tutor described two essentially different types of applicant:

[those] from grammar-type schools who have six to ten O levels, achieved through rote learning, and two Es at A level... and those from comprehensives or sixth-form colleges with indifferent O levels but very good grades at A level.

Possibly to bring such problems into perspective, a number of polytechnic tutors recorded that at O level they looked only at the number passed and ignored the grades obtained. University tutors stressed the importance of the applicant's breadth of achievement although some looked particularly for English and mathematics. Others sought 'a good mix of arts and sciences', while pointing out that they did not show 'bias against applicants who did not offer this'. Some university tutors expected high grades in subjects related to the course being applied for, a few adding that they were prepared to accept 'very low O-level grades in the accompanying passes'. Others considered that 'range and good grades – ones and twos' were essential. Making O-level mathematics an essential requirement had been considered by at least one university arts faculty since it was now necessary for some major career areas. The policy had not been adopted but the provision of a 'remedial' mathematics class remained under consideration.

Employers and public examinations at 16 +

As was made clear earlier, the information concerning the use made of examinations by employers was gathered in a parallel study conducted under the auspices of the University of Reading (Jones, 1983). Although there was close cooperation between the projects and it was possible, for example, to ensure that areas of particular interest were included in the employer questionnaire, the essentially different nature of the selection and screening process for employment when contrasted with that for a continuation of education renders formal comparisons inappropriate. Further changes in economic and social conditions which have affected the recruitment position over the period of the study may also mean that the information is ephemeral.

Where possible the information gained from employers which relates primarily to recruitment from school sixth forms, sixth-form colleges and colleges of further education is considered in Chapter III. Most recruitment for 'professional and management' positions comes into this category. Where matters are less specific or of universal application they are included in this chapter.

The year 1981, when the employers' survey was conducted, was a year in which company closure was common and overall recruitment was more than offset by redundancy. A common response to economic difficulty has been to cut back on recruitment and school leavers have proved particularly vulnerable. In the long term, of course, the survival of some organizations may depend on maintaining an even flow of young recruits and spreading training costs over time. In times of stringency less measured strategies prevail.

The employer sample inevitably included organizations not recruiting school leavers. There were a number of reasons for this, such as the level of technical skill required from recruits, the nature of the operation in which the organization was involved (such as the use of 'dangerous' processes) and an extensive use of shift work. When such non-recruiters were eliminated it was clear that school-leaver recruitment was declining rapidly. When compared with an 'average' recruitment figure for earlier years, recruitment for 1980 had decreased by some 5 per cent and that for the year of the survey by a further 23 per cent. Despite such dramatic reductions a large majority of the organizations, almost nine in every ten, had retained a policy of recruiting school leavers.

There were considerable differences in recruitment patterns for the various types of employment.* From every perspective, however, 'clerical and sales' formed the largest single area of recruitment.†

Of employers concentrating recruitment activity in the 16 + age range only six in every hundred were not recruiting some clerical and sales employees whereas the proportion recruiting operatives was under 40 per cent. The apparent hierarchy of recruitment opportunities was thus headed by 'clerical and sales' positions and was followed, at something like half the frequency, by the categories 'skilled manual', 'technician' and 'operative'. Job opportunities were reduced most dramatically for the least skilled workers, the opportunity hierarchy closely following the pattern of qualifications and the apparent level of skills required for particular occupations.

Employers' academic requirements of young recruits were usually tied firmly to 'a good basic education', usually construed as a sound knowledge of English and arithmetic:

[We require] a basic knowledge of the three Rs. It is a condemnation of our education system today that there is a high percentage who cannot do a simple arithmetic test and some who cannot write. Too much attention is paid to unnecessary subjects.

They should have basic literacy and numeracy and be interested in learning and doing – they should not be looking for an escape from an unpleasant experience.

---

* Categories of industry included in the Reading survey were: 'basic' industry (energy and water), mining and heavy manufacture, metal/vehicle engineering, other manufacturing, construction, distributive and catering, transport and other communication, banking and insurance, general services.

† The Reading research categorized jobs within the following broad areas: professional and managerial, clerical and sales, technician, skilled manual, operative.

A 'continued interest in learning' was often included and more directly vocational requirements were listed by a small number of employers. Some vocational requirements such as 'basic office skills' or 'craft training' were fairly specific although others were more directed towards enthusiasm such as 'an interest in engineering' and a few were more wide-ranging, specifying items such as 'a knowledge of industry and its ways'. There were only minor differences in employers' requirements for recruits to the different categories of employment at these levels.

The non-academic attributes sought by employers covered a wide range of qualities and behaviours. In order of the frequency with which they were mentioned, these included:

> having a smart appearance/being clean and presentable
> being hard working/steady/reliable/well disciplined/enthusiastic/highly motivated
> being punctual
> being cheerful
> being courteous
> having basic common sense
> having good general knowledge
> having interpersonal skills/ability to communicate/social confidence
> being flexible
> showing initiative.

A few employers included attributes such as 'honesty', 'integrity' and 'loyalty' among those valued. Some went on to recommend that pupils should be prepared in the completion of application forms and performance at selection interviews.

For three categories of employment – clerical and sales, skilled manual and operative – the interview was felt to be the most important source of information about candidates. In recruitment to technical posts, however, the interview was displaced as the most important source by academic qualifications. Across these four categories of employment, examination results were ranked second in importance – though there were wide divergences between the employment categories concerning the priority given to the various sources of information. Academic qualifications were ranked as second in importance for recruitment to clerical and sales positions, third in selection of skilled manual workers and only as fifth in importance for the recruitment of operatives.

Employers' own application forms were consistently considered to rank second or third in importance as tools for recruitment to all four categories of employment. School references were also fairly consistently viewed, being ranked fourth overall in order of importance. Employers' detailed opinions concerning the value of school references were as variable as those previously recorded within the educational sector. Where employers always sought school references they typically used them to:

provide background information in many areas which [is] then followed up at interview... The... reference may not provide all the information which is required but this again is sought at interview.

Such employers expressed the hope that schools were:

... in a position, after knowing the student for a number of years, to give a fair and unbiased opinion ... When one considers the cost [of subsequent training] a company should be given initial information which is as accurate as possible so that [it] can select wisely – although one accepts that no-one is infallible in their judgement.

A number of employers, while making use of references in this way, confirmed that '... it is always kept in mind that such assessments are subjective ...' Some employers made only occasional use of school references while others rejected them as sources of useful information for a number of reasons:

Success at school is not always a predictor of our requirements.
[We] place little reliance on school references as they are often optimistic ... rather than factual ...
[We] have no confidence except for grammar ... and church schools ...
We rely on our own tests and judgements ...
The look in their eyes tells us more ...

Examinations were fairly consistently seen as 'essential' by almost half the employers recruiting to all categories of employment at 16 +. The proportion ranged from 54 per cent of those recruiting technicians to 40 per cent of those recruiting at operative level. Academic results were least sought in recruitment to skilled manual and operative posts. Qualifications were given rather more emphasis in the selection of clerical and sales staff but, where required, were usually seen as measures of general rather than job-specific abilities.

Some employers used their own tests to replace examination results. It was possible to identify two major functions for which such tests were used. The first was to establish basic educational competency or general ability through tests of numerical and verbal skills, general reasoning and intelligence. These were the most commonly used tests in recruitment to all categories of employment.

The second purpose in testing was to identify performance on task-related skills. Thus tests of clerical skills were frequently included when clerical and sales staff were being selected and tests of mechanical aptitude were used in the identification of suitable technicians and skilled manual workers. Although these tests were seen in a positive way as identifying potentially successful employees, naturally they also served to eliminate 'unsuitable' applicants from further consideration.

In the light of the variations in importance attached to examination results it is interesting to look at the level of qualifications sought by employers for the particular categories of employment. Again the picture was somewhat confused by diverse recruitment intentions within the employment categories: a single employer seeking technicians may require some with minimal qualification, some with qualifications gained in public examinations at 16 + and some with 18 + qualifications.

As has been stated, most recruitment at professional and managerial level involved a requirement for examination success at 18 +. What is perhaps more surprising is that large proportions of those recruiting to technical and clerical and sales positions also recorded a desire to recruit from this population and some employers still recorded some recruitment of this type at skilled manual level.

The lowest level of academic qualification was identified as 'on a CSE or GCE course'. It was only in respect of skilled manual and operative posts that such a level of qualification was accepted by more than a small proportion of employers, although at operative level some employers considered even this minimal academic qualification unnecessary. Within technical and clerical and sales categories the level most commonly required of recruits was the possession of at least three O levels at grade C or better. For technician recruitment this represented the typical level of employer demand, being required by twice as many employers as all other levels combined. For posts in the clerical and sales category, almost as many employers recorded a desired level of one to three O levels and grades below C were rarely acceptable. Small numbers of employers seeking to recruit skilled manual workers also required some applicants to have these levels of academic achievement although, much more commonly, three or more CSE passes at grade 3 or better were desired.

One might expect the acceptability of CSE grade 1 as a replacement for GCE O-level grades A, B or C to vary inversely with the number and level of O-level passes sought. This was not universally so, although some confirmation for such a hypothesis could be found. Only one-fifth of those recruiting to professional and managerial positions, for example, considered CSE grade 1 to be 'acceptable as an O-level pass'. Those recruiting for technician posts, where a majority required three O levels, took a different stance, almost four in ten identifying a CSE grade 1 as acceptable. More than half of those recruiting for clerical and sales positions, where lower grade O levels were usually desired, accepted the equivalence of CSE grade 1. Those appointing school leavers to work at skilled manual and operative level, where CSE qualifications were respectively identified as appropriate and symbols of over-qualification, dramatically reversed this trend.

The equivalence of CSE grade 1 was accepted by less than a quarter of those seeking skilled manual workers and by only one in ten of those recruiting operatives. Perhaps such views owe as much to ignorance of the system, or at least of O-level examinations, as to a knowledge of the CSE.

Where academic requirements were expressed in terms of particular subjects, mathematics, English and science accounted for almost all the variation. Thus in recruitment to clerical and sales posts nine out of ten subject specifications were the paired 'English and mathematics'. More than eight in ten of the subjects required for technical posts were mathematics, science or English and only one in ten were 'technical' subjects.

It was only in recruitment to skilled manual vacancies that technical subjects achieved a reasonable measure of support, being specified at the rate of about one in five of the required subjects. While technical subjects were chosen more frequently than pure sciences, even here mathematics, English and the sciences together formed four-fifths of the subjects specified, seeming to confirm the commonly held belief that employers opt for familiar subjects construed as 'basics' even where relevant, and perhaps more pertinent, information is available from other sources.

This is not the place to explore possible relationships between academic performance in basic subjects under test and occupational skills in everyday use, but it does seem reasonable to ask if employers have clear and coherent ideas of the demands made in various occupational placements and how they might have a bearing on selection procedures.

Most employers offered several reasons for seeking particular academic qualifications. Many of those recruiting technicians said specific qualifications were formally necessary for professional advance or as a prerequisite for further training. These points featured much less frequently in connection with the three other categories of employment although they remained overall the most frequently recorded reasons for seeking academically qualified recruits. Employers recruiting to all types of employment tended to share the belief that examinations were both measures of intelligence and predictors of future performance. These were offered as the two major reasons for using examination results in the selection of clerical and sales staff. They were ranked as the first and third most common reasons in the selection of operatives, as second and third in the recruitment of skilled manual workers and as third and fourth in technician recruitment. Looking at 'prediction' somewhat differently, examination success was seen as 'necessary for successful job performance' by a significant proportion of respondents in connection with all categories of employment. In the selection of clerical and sales staff this rationale was placed fourth in priority. In other categories of 16 + recruitment it emerged as the fifth or sixth most important reason for requiring academic qualifications.

Further insight into the way in which employers make use of examination results came from the differential way in which they were used to screen out excess applicants in the various employment categories. Employers placed screening as the sixth most important factor in the recruitment of technical staff. The screening function was ranked third in the recruitment of clerical and sales staff, and for skilled manual and operative level selection it rivalled 'measures of intelligence' as the most frequently mentioned reason for using examination results. Although almost a third of the employers said they applied academic criteria rigidly, particularly with respect to recruitment at 18+, those recruiting at 16+ were more likely to apply their rules flexibly.

These responses appear to support the view that employers use examinations where success is necessary to permit recruits to obtain further useful qualifications. Apart from this, examination results are predominantly used as an easy way of reducing the large numbers of applicants to manageable proportions.

As in the education sector, interviews were the major means of assessing the non-academic qualities of applicants. Some of the qualities looked for at interview showed a remarkable consistency across all types of employment. Among these, some – such as those relating to appearance and cooperativeness – were sought by most employers while others – such as those connected with family background and previous experience – were considered by fewer employers recruiting to all categories. 'Social acceptability' was a quality which was similarly stable across all categories of employment and the number of employers seeking evidence of it at interview placed it in an intermediate position.

Other qualities showed marked variation in the number of employers recording their importance for different categories of work. 'Academic potential' and 'initiative/leadership potential' were, for example, looked for by many employers when recruiting technicians but by steadily fewer when clerical and sales staff, skilled manual workers and operatives were being interviewed.

This pattern was almost totally reversed in the case of 'physical well being' although rather more employers recorded its importance in the selection of technicians than did so for sales and clerical staff. Such apparently clear distinctions in the qualities required from applicants for different types of vacancy mask the issue of how these might be measured in an inevitably brief interview. Although those interviewing for industrial vacancies will usually, at least in large companies, have had some preparation for the task this is by no means always so. The criteria used to identify such qualities are not readily apparent nor are the techniques by which such criteria might be put into operation. These issues are returned to in the following chapter, particularly in connection with selection for places in higher education.

Summary and discussion

Chapter II has focused upon the use made of 16 + examinations to control access to GCE A-level courses, other non-advanced courses and to employment.

Within the school sector some interesting differences were apparent in the range of courses on offer in the different types of institution. Independent schools, for example, were shown to have generally smaller sixth forms and to offer a more limited curriculum than maintained schools. In colleges of further education the variety of courses was at its greatest and such colleges, in general, seemed able to respond more rapidly to changing curriculum needs than was possible within schools and sixth-form colleges. In all sectors shortages of resources and lack of facilities were said to be limiting the range of provision.

The proportion of schools and colleges claiming to offer open access to courses was small and many still appeared, in practice, to apply some form of academic bar. In particular, few courses were open to those whose qualifications placed them at, or just above, the national average in ability. It was clear that, even within the educational system, CSE grade 4 has yet to be accepted as an indication of average performance. Perhaps the concept of a national average, although much discussed, is too large to be grasped by even an informed audience. Outside educational circles the conception of 'average' owes much more to individual experience than to any national reality. Choice of courses appeared to be further restricted for some students by the grant aid policy adopted by local authorities.

The excess of applicants to places in schools and colleges has resulted in an inflation of the qualifications required for entry. It is therefore debatable how far qualifications were inherently necessary for given courses and how far they were being used simply to control numbers. Applicants were certainly expected to produce levels of qualifications which varied considerably from institution to institution. This was true even of applications to nationally validated courses with formally defined entry criteria. Seen from one perspective, such procedures were creating an untapped pool of talent within the country.

Many users of public examinations appear singularly ill-informed. They do not know, or are unconvinced by, explanations of the relationship between GCE O level and CSE. They do not know, or are doubtful of, efforts to ensure continuity of examination standards over time and between boards. They do not know or are unwilling to consider that Mode III has any validity, yet are ready to condemn traditional modes of examining for irrelevance. Since 16 + examinations retain their power to affect the lives of the majority of school leavers, it is important to find ways of improving understanding and practice at this level.

Lack of confidence in the examination system often arises from misunderstanding. Where value is attributed, it is to those (GCE) examinations which could clearly be traced back to their familiar and 'respectable' School Certificate origins. Any hint of newness, albeit of some 20 years' standing in the case of the CSE examination, generates doubts of fairly fundamental proportions.

Such widespread and uniform assertions of the value of the traditional raise questions about the acceptability of a common examination at 16 + quite separate from those related to its structure and conduct. However, they do cast as much light upon the somewhat equivocal response to proposals for change.

The two examinations at 16 + remain the most potent reflection of a pupil's educational experience at the end of the period of compulsory schooling. In order to provide this service with some sensitivity there is a need, within a decentralized system of education, for considerable diversity of provision. Tensions inevitably arise when examinations are also seen as a means of comparing applicants' potential.

It was not only among employers that English and mathematics performance was identified as crucial in this respect. For each group of users these basic subjects appeared as essential factors among the selection criteria.

The perceived utility of such a subject core extended through the whole of post-16 education and employment.

Nevertheless, levels of entry qualification identified as essential by some institutions were explicitly rejected elsewhere. Further and more specific research would be needed to explore the relationship between what serves as evidence of a candidate's readiness for a course, the intellectual demands the course actually presents and the effect of different admission policies upon the subsequent end-of-course qualifications received by accepted candidates.

The cool reception frequently given to information from an applicant's previous school suggests that transition at 16+ is identified by many as an opportunity for a 'fresh start' at entry to employment or to a new educational sector. However, it also raises doubts about the attention that would be paid to more extensive, accurate and appropriate information. Some respondents explicitly confirmed this, although there was obviously some conflict between the value given to the concept of the 'fresh start' and the importance attached to the idea of progression. The evidence provided by schools and colleges tended to throw into question the possibility of a genuinely fresh start at 16+ while not offering any great measure of practical support for the aim of progression.

Where applicants were tested, and this was most likely to take place in colleges of further education, the tests were sometimes used as another barrier to admissions rather than for purposes of guidance or identification of educational need. Interestingly, they were most often used to assess, once again, basic skills in English and to a lesser extent mathematics. Such use seems to confirm a lack of confidence in the ability of public examinations to inform on such basic skills. The importance attached to English and mathematics qualifications at 16+ was underlined by the existence in most institutions of policies designed to ensure that students should obtain some certification in these areas.*

In contrast with this minimal core of qualification, admission to some A-level courses required specific subjects and levels of performance from entrants. Although there were clear subject patterns, with mathematics setting the most stringent requirements, there was also variation between different types of institution. Thus a high level of qualification was most likely to be demanded by grammar schools and least likely to be insisted

---

* For a critique of the way in which O-level English language is used see Torbe *et al.* (1981).

upon by colleges of further education. An essentially similar subject pattern was found across the range of institutions.

Another aspect of comparability, that of the relationship between CSE and GCE, was also problematic, though strongly held views were not always supported with rational argument. Few respondents showed a clear understanding of the basis of comparability between the two examinations; that is, the comparison of a common population rather than a common experience. Differences in content, teaching approach and methods of assessment were seen by some as undermining practical equivalence. The result is that candidates offering grade 1 CSE are frequently regarded less favourably than candidates offering a grade A, B or C at O level. In some subject areas, notably mathematics, the distinctions were expressly defined by respondents. It is a small consolation that the problems arise from a misunderstanding of the target population of the two examinations and the overlapping nature of the boundary which separates them. A number of those contributing to the research pointed out that neither examination was a particularly good predictor of subsequent A-level performance. Nevertheless, both examinations were generally used in this way and some admissions tutors in higher education also considered them as most important evidence of potential.

Although many employers suggested that formal qualifications played a relatively small part in their selection procedures, it was clear that examinations were seen as valuable indicators of intelligence and as predictors of future performance. Employers were also particularly interested in performance in English and arithmetic and some wanted evidence of scientific achievement. It is not easy to justify the limitation of value in educational experience to performance in English and mathematics across such a wide spectrum of employment and educational opportunity. Nevertheless, this study has revealed that many users take performance in these subjects as a sufficient basis upon which to judge 'general ability', possibly in response to their own failure to establish more specific requirements. Some evidence was accrued to support this latter view. The further elaboration of a candidate's performance in English and mathematics through tests used by employers and further education colleges may underline the status of these subjects, or perhaps reflect the misleading simplicity with which such tests can be obtained or constructed.

For some occupations examinations were needed to allow access to further professional training but they as often represented a relatively easy means of reducing the number of candidates requiring more detailed scrutiny. Indeed, where the number of applicants greatly exceeds the number of places it is difficult to envisage a readily acceptable and less blunt alternative instrument. Change would presumably require a marked re-orientation of selection criteria towards the skills and knowledge required to take a course or to fill a job. Although schools, colleges and employers frequently claim to resist the use of qualifications as a crude screen and to 'take account of the individual' it is quite evident that movement towards a more imaginative and sensitive use of examination results is long overdue.

While employers voiced their opinion that there were too many boards, too many papers, and too much variety to comprehend, it was only within the educational area that a few selectors 'weighted' their academic entrance criteria for board or syllabus. A study such as this cannot hope fully to explore the relationship between needs and curriculum diversity. However, findings did indicate that those within education, although supporting a reduction in variety, would not seek to eliminate it.

Whereas those in education were usually satisfied with the educational achievement of the applicants they received this was less likely to be true of employers. Such differences may, of course, be due to differences in expectation, but in view of the increasing proportion of each cohort remaining at school or moving to other educational institutions it is quite possible that employers have actually been presented with fewer and fewer 16-year-old applicants who have shown any marked degree of scholastic success. If this is so then it is hardly surprising that their expectations in this respect are confounded. Perhaps the increased pressure upon the young to grasp any early employment opportunity will reverse this trend.

III. The use made of 18 + examinations

Public examinations at 18 + and 16 + share many features but there are a series of characteristics which clearly divide them. Status is lent to A level because it provides a passport to the more prestigious areas of higher education. Reactions to the last attempt to reform its structure clearly demonstrated how close in many minds was the link between A levels and ideals of academic excellence. There are also marked differences in the numbers of individuals who are involved in these two major cycles of public examinations.

The comparative reduction in numbers at 18 + is not matched by an increase in the proportion who 'survive to and beyond selection'. Higher education has traditionally been the sector where the maximum of resources have been allocated to the smallest number. Former ideals of higher education as exemplified in the Robbins Report (Committee on Higher Education, 1963),* despite bringing a sustained expansion in provision, have done little to alter this. Those that survive are drawn very unequally from different areas of society, although A. H. Halsey *et al.* (1980) have demonstrated clearly that inequity is not a major feature of 18 + selection but 'very largely a consequence of earlier decisions in the educational process'. They also showed that the differential use of educational resources was not limited to higher education but that it characterized further education even in the area of part-time provision.

Although higher education is for the smallest numbers, it is within colleges of further education and in polytechnics and universities that the provision of courses reaches its maximum complexity. This effect is partly due to the instrumental nature of some of the courses, since many become vocational. Others, while not offering direct vocational paths, also concentrate – in the name of scholarship – more and more upon less and less. Much complexity is due to the dominant educational model in which increasingly varied and narrow specialisms branch off from the basic

* See also Robbins (1980).

trunk extending through primary and much of secondary schooling. The resultant diversity has given rise to a series of 'guide books' to higher education as well as to research such as that carried out by W. A. Reid (1974).

This chapter explores the way in which public examinations are used to control access to this variety and to the alternative track of employment at the age of 18. For the sake of simplicity the term 'university' is used to include schools and colleges of a university and schools of medicine and dentistry where these are autonomous. The Universities of Oxford and Cambridge are, because of their very different selection procedures, explored separately. The information from Oxford and Cambridge was collected through discussions with the admissions tutors of twelve colleges and the administrative officers of the two universities. Inevitably a more detailed picture emerged of the procedures they adopted. To give a full account of this within a chapter exploring selection throughout further and higher education would distort the overall balance. Thus while the chapter includes a section exploring the implications which the admissions procedures at Oxford and Cambridge have for the system as a whole, the review appears in full as Appendix B.

The term 'polytechnic' includes a small number of colleges of higher education and where colleges of further education are described, the information applies only to their advanced courses as designated by the Department of Education and Science. 'Degree courses' include degree courses available in all types of institution. The Open University and the University College at Buckingham were not included in the survey.

Range of provision

Differences in size are probably of less significance in determining the range of provision within a higher education institution than are the interests and enthusiasms of individuals and groups working within it. Courses within individual universities have historically been largely determined by tradition. In more recent time the range of provision has been loosely in the grip of the University Grants Committee (UGC), since it is through this body that the dispersal of centrally provided funding has occurred. Only in very recent times, and with the encouragement of the DES, has the UGC considered direct intervention in the size of courses and the balance between them (to meet an overall national strategy), to fall within its brief.* Even now, dramatic though some events have seemed within individual institutions, the effect has chiefly been to change the balance between courses rather than to bring about their demise.

Universities have retained their traditional self-regulating function in terms of course validation. Degree courses within colleges of higher education and polytechnics have been more centrally controlled through the Council for National Academic Awards (CNAA), although alternative validation – for example through a nearby university – has also been common. Other advanced courses have required a similar external validation and this has recently been accomplished through BEC and TEC (now BTEC).

It is doubtful, in any case, whether institutional provision is an important factor within the universities. Only if the suggestions of the mid-1970s for the development of local universities had been adopted would individual university provision have had much impact on selection. As it is the national pool of courses is open to all candidates.† However, the student populations in polytechnics and colleges of higher education have traditionally included a fairly large local element and the student body in colleges of further education is primarily, because of the nature of student grant aid, of neighbourhood origin. Here, then, the range of provision within a single institution must be of considerable significance to applicants.

A further factor, to which attention was drawn by a number of tutors in colleges of further education, was the part played by local authorities in determining both the range of courses offered and the entry criteria adopted in the selection of students. It was impossible to determine the potency of such influences, although reference to them was most frequently made in respect of newly established courses.

Less tangible market forces also apply, particularly at the foundation of a new course, since although general information will usually be available (syllabus and the names of tutors), applicants at this stage will rely heavily upon the published entry qualifications to judge the value of a course. In such cases the need to establish credibility may well cause the setting of

---

* It remains difficult to understand the rationale behind, for example, direct intervention in the allocation of places for medical courses, while 'student demand' has been allocated responsibility for features such as growth in social science courses and the standard of entry requirements in engineering.

† The annual DES Statistics and Awards confirm, however, a continuing differential uptake of places by region, with the southeast being over-represented. See, for example, the interpretation by Baylin (1983) or that of McDowell (1981).

higher entry qualifications than the course content would actually demand.

Equally intangible factors affect the viability of courses in higher education and, almost annually, lists appear of the 'most popular universities', the 'top ten polytechnics' and the popularity rating of particular areas of study. Given such diversity, it was necessary for the research to concentrate upon a small number of courses and to look at these in detail in only some institutions. The courses included in the study appear in Appendix A, Tables 5 and 6.

The variety of courses offered by further education colleges also ensured that entry procedures were determined at course level, although discussions with tutors revealed extensive cooperation between courses and the 'trading' of applicants whose qualifications rendered their placement more appropriate elsewhere. Entry procedures in higher education were most commonly determined at faculty, school or department level, the department being the determining body for two-thirds of all courses. Universities also provided a few examples of the transfer of applicants who failed to meet the conditions of their offers, to courses making rather less stringent demands. Within polytechnics a number of course tutors pointed out that their procedures were determined by the CNAA and this body, together with a 'course committee', shaped the admissions procedures.

The course committee was a body apparently unknown in universities. In no case within higher education was the selection of students determined solely by institutional requirements.

Information about the admissions procedures in particular universities and polytechnics was most commonly provided by an admissions tutor, although responses were also received from others, including directors of studies, heads of department and deans of faculty. In further education colleges the course tutor was the usual informant.

Number of applicants and size of course

Advanced courses in further education colleges typically included approximately thirty students. Although half the courses were undersubscribed or received just sufficient applicants to maintain the desired group size, the remainder received a surplus of candidates. The possible relationship between the number of applicants which a course received and the level of entry qualifications it demanded could not be tested statistically although there was no reason to expect that this should be different from that apparent in higher education. The pressure on places at its greatest represented eight applicants for every place. In approximately half of the courses all the applicants were interviewed. Almost all, in turn, received offers of places conditional upon achieving specific examination results. The use of 'unconditional offers', where a candidate is apparently given a place not tied to subsequent examination performance, was rare.

A typical polytechnic course consisted of rather more than fifty students and received over 250 applications for places. Over half of the applicants were interviewed and, in general, four-fifths received a conditional offer of a place on the course.

The remaining fifth received an unconditional offer. This would usually mean they had already gained the appropriate qualifications. In such instances, the use of the term 'unconditional' may seem incongruous, but it reflects guidelines laid down by the chief advisory body on university applications, the Universities Central Council on Admissions (UCCA).

University courses usually included about fifty students and typically attracted about 250 applicants. Approximately 100 of these were interviewed and some 200 made a conditional offer of a place. Unconditional offers were usually made to a maximum of ten applicants. No reference was made outside Oxford and Cambridge to 'matriculation' offers, where the offer of a place is conditional upon the applicant gaining just two A-level passes. The two-A-level standard relates to the minimum entry requirement to university associated with the original concept of matriculation. The gaining of matriculation status normally carried no implication of a place. The subject of offers will be further explored later in this chapter.

When the number of applicants to particular degree courses was looked at in detail it became clear that some courses – almost irrespective of where they were sited – received large numbers of applicants, whereas others received very few. University courses concerned with business management, English, law and medicine most frequently recorded more than a thousand applicants, whereas combined honours arts courses and combined honours in language and literature commonly attracted under twenty-five candidates.

No polytechnic course recorded less than fifty applicants and only biological sciences, mathematics and statistics and physics included individual courses with less than one hundred applicants. Courses receiving over 500 applicants were accountancy, biological sciences, business studies, civil engineering, and electrical and electronic engineering.

The number of applicants to all types of institutions appeared relatively static and no major differences were recorded between the year of the study and the previous year. The UCCA statistics for the year of the survey recorded an increase of approximately 4 per cent in the number of United Kingdom applicants compared with the previous year but indicated that in some subjects there were substantial decreases in the numbers of applicants (notably civil engineering and biological sciences) and for others there were substantially more applicants than in the previous year (particularly computing and drama).* Most courses, whatever their content, recorded a relatively stable application rate although there were a few courses (computer science, mathematics, physics, sociology and geology) where a single institution recorded a doubling in the number of applicants in the year of study.

THE STANDARD OF QUALIFICATIONS HELD BY APPLICANTS

Seven out of ten tutors in universities and colleges of further education agreed that the standard of applicants was unchanged in comparison with the previous year, while in polytechnics the majority of tutors considered that there had been an improvement. In no area of higher and further education did the proportion of tutors considering that there had been a decrease in the quality of applicants exceed one in twenty. Although it might be considered likely that those recording a decline in the level of qualifications among applicants would be drawn from those areas currently suffering from a shortage of candidates, this did not appear to be the case; nor were such views prevalent within any institution or type of institution.

The admissions tutors of some university courses in, for example, accountancy, chemistry, physics and geology tended to perceive an improvement, whereas in biology, economics, law and medicine tutors felt there had been no change. However, in no discipline did a majority of university tutors consider that there had been an increase in the qualification level of applicants.

Standards of admission in many polytechnics were judged to be rising in terms of the grades required at A level and the rejection of 'weaker candidates'. One electrical and electronic engineering course said it had 'increased the requirement every year for the last three'.

Where university admissions tutors recorded that there had been an improvement in the level of qualifications held by candidates some said that this had made little or no difference to the offers made to candidates. Most,

---

* 'Substantial change' was linked to both percentage change and total number of applicants involved.

however, confirmed that the effect had been to increase the level of grades required. Specific examples give some indication of the extent of the changes:

General offer was raised from CCD to BCC. (university, sociology course)

Standard offer has risen from CCC to BCC. (university, history course)

Offer has increased from CCE to BCE. (university, physics course)

Some tutors also reported that they were able to apply the entry requirements 'more rigidly' and others suggested that the major effect was to 'increase the rejection rate'. Interestingly, in those few cases recording a decline in the level of qualifications offered by candidates the effect on offers was identical – it led to the raising of the required conditions by approximately one point. In polytechnics the few tutors claiming a decrease in the level of traditional candidate qualifications had turned to other sources, using for example TEC Certificate and Diploma qualifications for recruitment to a School of Architecture.

University and polytechnic courses were likely to include less than one in ten mature students whereas the proportion was commonly twice this among advanced courses in further education colleges. The selection criteria usually involved a reduction in the level of formal academic requirements and a greater emphasis on experience. In a small fraction of institutions mature students were expected to take a test of some sort. Special matriculation requirements for mature students were reported by some university tutors although the age at which applicants were considered 'mature' varied from 21 years, to over 25 (at which age a change in student status occurs as far as grant aid is concerned). Typical comments were as follows:

... a special examination can be set. An interview is essential and this can be lengthy. (university, mathematics course)

The interview is more formal and is given greater significance than with A-level candidates. (university, chemical engineering course)

A special committee decides on the qualification required if a departmental interview has been satisfactory. (university, French course)

Occasionally a one-year pre-entry course was arranged with a nearby college of further education and some courses required 'evidence of recent academic activity'.

Information about applicants

University admissions tutors had standardized information made available through UCCA but, at the time of the survey, both polytechnics and colleges of further education relied upon their own application forms as the major initial source of information about candidates. A central clearing scheme essentially modelled on UCCA and probably sharing its computer facilities and expertise is currently being introduced for polytechnics.

The origins and duties inherent in centralized clearing for universities are described in the offical guide (UCCA, 1980):

> The Universities Central Council on Admissions was set up in 1961 by the universities of the United Kingdom. Their object was principally to solve the problems caused by increasing numbers of multiple applications i.e. from candidates who applied in the same year to different universities and accepted offers from each. The consequent withdrawals, and the scramble to refill places in the last fortnight before term began were unfair to both candidates and universities and drove the latter, with strong encouragement from the schools, towards a cooperative solution. The duty of the Central Council is to enable the business of admissions to undergraduate courses in all the constituent United Kingdom universities to be dealt with in an orderly manner which allows each candidate freedom to make a responsible choice and each university freedom to select its own students ...

A description of the admissions procedure provided by UCCA runs to some 35 A4 pages and the Council provides guidelines for selectors (e.g. UCCA, 1982) as well as for the candidate. The origin of much of this information is the Standing Conference on University Entrance (SCUE) and UCCA was described to the researchers as 'a glorified postbox' for the 'four-and-a-half million pieces of paper floating round the country'.

The candidate application form used by UCCA collects personal details (such as sex, marital status, age, country of residence and origin, nationality and name and occupation of parent or guardian); name and address; choice of university and course; educational history; experience; proposed career and interests; examinations passed and to be taken; and a 'confidential statement by a referee'. Since this last item provides essential academic and non-academic information for selectors, the instructions for its completion are provided in full in Appendix C.

Suggestions that this last aspect of the UCCA form could be completed using computer-accessible five-point rating scales were apparently met by 'a united howl of protest from both schools and universities'. It was accepted that even the structure provided by existing headings was 'pretty unpopular in schools' because 'they like the freedom to write in their own way'. Nevertheless, some schools already collected much of the information required for the UCCA form in a graded format, details then being transferred in the continuous prose style prescribed by the form. One such example recorded,

a range of assessments of potential, academic performance, personal qualities and social abilities on a five point scale, together with extended comment in amplification from each subject tutor. (comprehensive school)

Two specimen pages from the document appear in Appendix C.

The confidentiality of the UCCA form was not broached by admissions tutors. However, although the form is designated as 'confidential' by its originators, some schools no longer treat it as such. Some local authorities have also questioned whether the form can remain confidential where school records are open to students and parents. In such circumstances the predicting of A-level performance, which is currently an essential element of the form, will undoubtedly become an issue for increasing debate.

University tutors made few criticisms of the UCCA form and, although a small number criticized the inclusion of the occupation of parent or guardian, many more recorded that they found this information valuable, claiming that it enabled them to adjust their approach when interviewing the applicant. A number of polytechnic tutors expressed their wish to receive application information in a similar standardized form.

University and polytechnic departments often also collected information from candidates via their own forms. While there was some duplication, much of the content was concerned specifically with detail relevant to selection for the course involved. Some forms with searching questions on interests and experiences almost constituted a test of the applicant.

The way in which a departmental application form may be used to provide 'test material' was illustrated by one university school of architecture. After seeking career intention and comment on recently visited buildings of note the questionnaire ended:

PLEASE SUBMIT WITH THIS QUESTIONNAIRE

1 A picture map (not just a plan) showing the route from your present place of abode to the nearest Post Office.
2 *Either*
A sketch of the building in which you live and give a short appraisal of it as architecture.
or
A sketch of your own room (or the one you share) together with a further sketch showing proposed improvements to it including furniture and furnishings.

3 A short appreciation (approx. 200 words) of any work of fine art or applied art which you have recently seen, setting it in its present-day context.
You may if you wish add anything you would like us to know or to discuss at a possible interview.

More than nine out of ten further education college tutors received basic information concerning the applicant's expected examination results, an assessment of suitability for the course and an assessment of personal qualities for those applicants arriving directly from school. Schools were rather less likely to offer the official school record of applicants to advanced courses than had been the case for applicants to non-advanced courses.

Admissions tutors in polytechnics and universities had remarkably similar views about the importance of the various items of information provided on applicants. Nine in ten considered that the information on the applicant's personal qualities was important or very important, half recorded that information on the health of the candidate was important or very important and a third attached a similar importance to the position of their institution in the applicant's order of choice (apparent from the UCCA form). The importance attached to examination performance at 16+ has been explored in the previous chapter and there were quite marked differences between tutors in their view of predictions of performance at 18+. Whereas half of the admissions tutors in universities considered that the predicted examination results presented very important information, this view was offered by less than a quarter of those selecting for polytechnic courses. Conversely, one in ten polytechnic tutors and one in twenty university tutors felt that the predicted results were without importance for selection.

UCCA has observed that, in general, schools understandably 'tended towards the generous' and that 'predicted results were often higher than actual results'. R. J. L. Murphy (1980) confirmed:

a definite tendency, on the part of ... teachers, to over-predict the A-level grades by an average of one grade per candidate [per subject] ...

The point must be made that teacher estimates of grade in Murphy's study were, however moderate the association, better predictors of A-level grades than were candidates' O-level performances.

The rather weak correlation between A-level grades and subsequent degree performance has already been referred to in Chapter I (Choppin, 1973) and attention was again drawn to this aspect across a range of disciplines by a number of tutors:

There is no correlation between A-level results and first degree results in the applied sciences. Good A-level performance indicates a good memory and/or good examination technique. It does not necessarily mean a good ability to apply knowledge to practical matters. It could mean that the school concerned is particularly competent in tutoring pupils in the A-level system, beyond which they become out of their depth. While A-level results are inevitably part of the selection procedures and have to carry more weight where a candidate cannot be interviewed, the correlation between A-level grades and final results is depressingly low in French and every effort has to be made to use other evidence in selection ...

I dislike the present system of admissions to university where candidates are generally given provisional places conditional on their reaching certain grades in A level, which creates a double hurdle for them. Moreover I am not convinced of the value of A-level grades as indicators of suitability for university-level study. I would prefer to be able to select candidates by interview with the help of detailed confidential reports from their schools and to be able to make all offers unconditional ...

Both O- and A-level examination results correlate poorly with subsequent degree performance. The one subject that is generally indicative of success in the social sciences (whether mathematically oriented or not) is mathematics – the nearest thing to an intelligence test. I would favour the use of sophisticated intelligence tests to supplement the O- and A-level results.

Other tutors, while recognizing the dilemma, took a rather more instrumental view of the problem:

While there is not necessarily a direct correlation between A-level results and ultimate Ll.B. degree results nevertheless, generally speaking, something of the order of 3 A levels (10 points), to 2 A levels (8 points) is usually needed to stand a chance of coping with the demands imposed by a Law degree.

I am well aware that GCE grades are very imperfect predictors of subsequent academic success (in mathematics and psychology) but I am quite clear:
a that they are definitely significantly better than nothing:
b that they are closer to an objective measure of the candidate's ability ... than any kind of internally assessed profile ...
c that the absence of examinations in clearly laid down syllabuses *not* under the control of schools would lead to a gross deterioration of academic standards – and goodness knows they are low enough already.

Many admissions tutors in higher education used the 'points system' where A-level grades are given a numerical value (A = 5, down to E = 1) and added together. AAA thus becomes 15 and matriculation standard is 2 (EE). Entry is then set at a particular numerical value. The system used thus approximates to the 'grade-point' system so commonly used in the

United States. Although offering a bureaucratic solution, the practice makes statistical nonsense of the grades gained and effectively hides much information claimed by selectors to be of value. Where specific levels of performance in a core subject are required, for example, these will be masked by the addition. The points system was described by an opponent as a 'classic hoax' which, while purporting to suggest a needed level of intellect, is 'simply an expression of market forces'. A number of tutors were unable to describe offers other than in terms of 'points'.

Interdepartmental differences in the importance attached to predictions of examination results within the universities were in general slight. In computer science, law and mathematics the majority of tutors attaching great importance to predicted results was, however, very much larger than in other disciplines.

Interviewing

Where not all the applicants were interviewed, a range of criteria was applied in the selection of suitable candidates. There was considerable agreement between polytechnics and universities about the type of applicant who would be interviewed. The most frequently adopted policy, used by up to half of admission tutors, selected the 'most promising' candidates using aspects such as the predicted outcome of public examination and references. A third of tutors selected the 'borderline' candidates for closer scrutiny, those whose results were less certain or about whom some query arose in references. Also included in this selection would be mature students and others offering unusual qualifications or an unusual combination of qualifications.

A small proportion of tutors invited all mature applicants to interview; this was rather more likely to take place for mature applicants to polytechnics than for those to universities. In a few subject areas, notably art and design, medicine and dentistry, interviewing generally involves only the most promising candidates. Where all candidates were interviewed it was clear that, in some cases at least, the 'interview' consisted solely of a visit to the institution.

Some tutors pointed out that the present interviewing pattern was not necessarily adopted from choice:

> I would ideally like to interview all good students. This would mean interviewing some 300 + students – we do not have the resources to do this ... All students are invited to visit the university to meet staff and students and discuss the course and other facilities offered by the university. (accountancy)

The seriousness with which some tutors viewed the interview was also recorded:

It would be helpful if schools were aware that in giving their own mock-examinations priority over invitations for interview they may be reducing the chances of their students gaining university entrance in popular subjects. The reason for this is that with the current application of reduced quotas especially in subjects like English, the later the interview the less likely it is that there will be any places left.

The number of candidates interviewed appeared to vary little between degree courses. But when this number was looked at in relation to the number of applications received it became clear that in university courses where the numbers were high – notably in business management, English and law – there was a marked reduction in the proportion of applicants interviewed. The same was not apparent in polytechnics where the number interviewed showed a direct relationship with the number of applicants.

PURPOSE OF THE INTERVIEW

The interest shown by the candidate in the subject or subjects to be studied was rated as 'very important' by a majority of all tutors. Factors rated as 'important' by a majority in all types of institution were the reasons for choosing the department or institution, power of oral expression, temperament and the applicant's intended career. University tutors were least interested in career factors, and a minority of tutors in English, French, history, mathematics and sociology considered the career intention of candidates unimportant. Rather more surprisingly, these views were also shared by a majority of the tutors recruiting to chemistry, economics, law and physics where courses could have more direct vocational implications.

Where temperament was seen as important, aspects such as 'motivation' and 'determination' were most commonly mentioned. 'Self-confidence', 'enthusiasm', 'reliability' and 'ability to communicate' were recorded as necessary qualities across a wide range of courses whereas 'independence', 'curiosity', 'imagination' and 'flexibility' were seldom nominated. Not all social skills were equally welcomed: 'We dislike slippery "lower deck lawyer" types, i.e. shop steward types...'. (university, medicine)

Tutors from the different types of institutions varied in the value they placed upon the applicant's likely contribution to the general life of the institution. Whereas the majority of tutors in further education colleges and polytechnics considered this unimportant, a majority of university tutors thought otherwise. There was, however, a virtual consensus concerning the irrelevance of a candidate's leisure interests, though there were notable exceptions in university courses such as medicine, dentistry and chemical and civil engineering. A majority of those recruiting to medicine and dentistry, unlike those working in any other discipline, also placed great importance on the candidate's temperament and health.

While polytechnic admissions tutors agreed in general with their colleagues in universities on the important aspects of an applicant's temperament, a number were also concerned with the graduate's ability to survive after the course:

We are interested in the capacity to make the transition to higher education – evidence of initiative, independence and persistence [but also] potential for industrial training when an academically 'weaker' candidate may have to perform outstandingly well in interview to get the job. (polytechnic, applied biology)

One university tutor reviewed the non-academic criteria which were of most concern:

I really believe that all students should spend three years working away from the educational system before they start higher education. We would then have mature, motivated students who we would not have to waste so much time upon simply encouraging them to have enough confidence, as people, to work and get the best from us and our courses. (university, art and design)

Perhaps inevitably, an overall majority of admissions tutors also agreed that it was very important to assess a candidate's 'academic aptitude' at interview, but it was noteworthy that while four out of five university admissions tutors considered that the primary purpose of the admissions procedure was to select the most academically able candidates, only four in ten of those recruiting to polytechnics felt the same way.

Conditions applied to course entry

Entry requirements to a course are usually set at a higher level than those required for admittance to the institution.

Formal academic entry requirements existed for all the courses and these were usually expressed as a minimum number of GCE O and A levels. The individual nature of the offer was emphasized by many tutors, as were the varying factors which were taken into consideration.

Our admissions procedure is very much geared to the individual applicant. The only general rule which may be applied is that average applicants will probably receive average offers, currently BCC. Above average applicants will receive low offers i.e. CCC down to DDD. Poor applicants will receive high offers or rejections. O levels are not always a significant factor, though applicants with a run of good O levels, i.e. A or B grades, will be looked at more favourably than applicants with poor O levels. (university, history)

Although some tutors pointed out that a shortage of applicants would have 'inevitable' consequences for the level of offers which could be made (viz. more stringent demands), none admitted that offers were routinely raised as the course places were taken up, a practice which had featured in a number of newspaper articles in the year of the survey.

Tutors often made a clear distinction between the 'offer' and what was (eventually) accepted:

We ask for two Bs from candidates taking only two A levels, but we often accept BC. From the three-A-level candidate we ask for BCD but often accept BDD or BCE. (university, English)

Where the 'points system' was used a typical example was:

Candidates must have nine points plus a satisfactory portfolio. We can then modify to allow five points exceptionally, and usually on compassionate grounds, but rarely go below seven points. (university, art and design)

One tutor pointed out that A-level entry was not always appropriate:

We do not specify the grade of A-level pass required for entry – in most cases this has proved to be a poor indicator of ability ... (polytechnic, education)

The threshold for 'unconditional offers' was, in many institutions, set at nine points (A B), although the grades usually had to be in specified subjects. In this case, occasionally candidates with CCD were also made unconditional offers. More often, no clear grade requirements were laid down other than 'satisfactory A levels' but it was clear that the unconditional offer was sometimes used to attract candidates who had also applied to Oxford and Cambridge.

Concrete examples of the way in which admissions procedures worked were obtained by an exploration of the level of qualifications held by first-year students.

A student representing the lowest level of qualification on an advanced course in a further education college typically held five GCE passes including one at A level. The average student on such courses usually had five GCE passes, with two subjects studied to A level, but only one passed. The most highly qualified advanced course student typically held at least five

GCE passes including two at A level. The highest level of qualification held by students on a quarter of the advanced courses included three A-level passes and overall, half of the courses contained students who met or exceeded the matriculation requirements for a university course.

There was necessarily, therefore, a considerable overlap in terms of qualification between students following courses in further education colleges and those studying in polytechnics. Almost half the polytechnic courses held students holding two grade E A-levels although such students were representative of the lowest level of qualification. Students with three A levels at grade A or B were recorded in a quarter of all polytechnic courses, covering twelve course areas ranging from accountancy to sociology and including electrical engineering, linguistics and mathematics.

The lowest level of student qualification typically recorded on a university course was three A levels at grade C or D. Students with two A levels at grade E were only recorded on three courses (and one of these noted that the student was a mature candidate), underlining the disparity between the matriculation requirement and the actual level of qualification necessary to gain admission. On two-thirds of the university courses studied, the highest level of student qualification was typically described as three A levels at grade A or B and admissions tutors of a small number of courses recorded the presence of students with four and even five A levels at grade A.

The differences between the entry requirements for equivalent advanced courses in different colleges of further education were not as wide as those found between non-advanced courses. The most significant differences were where some colleges specified a pass in a single A level as part of their entry requirements and others did not. Examples included courses leading to Higher National Diploma (HND) chemistry and HND building.*

Differences in the minimum entry qualifications within polytechnics and universities usually amounted to about one grade. Much larger differences were apparent when university and polytechnic minimum entry requirements were considered for courses of the same title. Thus, for entry to a polytechnic mathematics degree course, two grade E A-levels were often acceptable while the highest minimum entry requirement was set at CD. Most university mathematics courses, however, set their minimum entry at BC, while a number required three A levels and a few set their minimum level as three A levels at grade A or B. A similar pattern prevailed across most disciplines.

---

* A single A level is officially required for entry to an HND course.

QUALIFIED CANDIDATES NOT SELECTED FOR THE COURSE

A range of reasons were offered for not allowing otherwise qualified applicants entry to degree courses. The most common of these was 'a very bad headteacher's report'. Aspects which were identified as particularly likely to lead to rejection were 'a bad attitude', 'an unsuitable personality', 'having a character detrimental to the studies of others', 'unacceptable social behaviour' and being 'a trouble maker'. A 'suspect performance' or a 'very bad attitude' at interview were often used to confirm the confidential report and a number of tutors pointed out that a candidate would often be called to interview even after a bad report. Emotional or mental instability, weak personality and serious psychological problems were also seen as grounds for rejection and a number of tutors included physical and sensory disability as a reason for refusing a place. One tutor complained 'The university health policy on disabled people is discriminatory'.

The inability of those with 'severe physical handicap' to cope with the 'Victorian building' in which the course was accommodated and to 'undertake a full practical course with fieldwork' were also cited as reasons for rejection. 'Poor motivation' was quite commonly given as a reason for excluding a qualified applicant and this was in some cases associated with 'applications made under parental pressure'. A final group of reasons were associated with conviction for a serious crime.

THE EQUIVALENCE OF CSE GRADE 1

The use of 16 + qualifications for 18 + admissions was outlined in Chapter II. Except in a tiny minority of cases, CSE grade 1 was accepted as equal to a GCE grade C or above in the same subject. Only in the university sector did the proportion of admissions tutors refusing to accept CSE grade 1 reach one in twenty. Those rejecting the equivalence of CSE grade 1 were fairly evenly scattered through both courses and institutions.

THE ACCEPTABILITY OF ALTERNATIVE QUALIFICATIONS TO CSE AND GCE

Tutors were asked to indicate whether they would accept or reject specified alternative examinations as appropriate qualifications for admission. Clearly, not all had been confronted with the issue and some were unfamiliar with certain qualifications. A common response, therefore, was to avoid the question. Sometimes as many as half the respondents offered no answer about a particular examination. More than a third of all tutors offered no answer to the question about qualifications certificated by the City and Guilds of London Institute (CGLI), the Royal Society of Arts (RSA) and the Open University. Qualifications validated by BEC and

TEC were treated in the same way by more than a third of university tutors and, more unexpectedly, BEC courses produced a non-response from more than a third of tutors in further education colleges.

There were, however, clear differences between institutions concerning the acceptability of alternative qualifications. BEC and TEC validated courses (together with ONC) were most readily accepted by polytechnic tutors, and TEC and ONC were deemed similarly acceptable for advanced courses in further education colleges. These last two qualifications were seen as appropriate by nine out of ten tutors in both types of institution. Three out of four tutors in polytechnics, and about two-thirds of those in further education, accepted BEC awards for entry purposes. Between a half and three-quarters of university admissions tutors accepted that BEC, TEC and ONC were appropriate for course entry. RSA courses, although following the same general pattern, were received with nothing like the same degree of approval. Such qualifications were accepted by around one in five of polytechnic tutors, by one in ten of those in further education, and by less than one in twelve university admissions tutors.

CGLI certificates were most readily accepted in further education colleges, where two-thirds of tutors considered them appropriate alternatives to 16 + qualifications. This proportion was halved in polytechnics and only one in ten of the university tutors accepted CGLI certificates.

The most universally acceptable alternative qualification was OND which almost all tutors in further education colleges and polytechnics found acceptable and which was declared to be a suitable alternative to GCE and CSE by more than three-quarters of those controlling university admissions. There were links apparent between acceptable alternatives and course content and these largely followed predictable lines. For example BEC qualifications were the most widely accepted alternative qualification for admission to business management degree courses. What was less easy to understand was an apparent rejection of all alternatives by tutors in a few institutions.

Tutors from all sectors identified other qualifications which they would accept. Examples of these were professional qualifications and foundation courses, accepted in polytechnics – although these in some cases offered only partial exemption – and the International Baccalaureate, 'Scottish Highers' and HND/HNC accepted in universities. Colleges of further education added no new qualification to those accepted elsewhere. No tutor included CEE on the list of acceptable courses, although the UCCA 'Notes for University Selectors' suggests that grades 1 to 3 of CEE 'should be given the same recognition as is currently given to grade 1 of CSE'.

(These notes also offer guidance on the equivalence of all other United Kingdom qualifications.)

THE EFFECTS OF SYLLABUS, BOARD AND MODE ON ENTRY PROCEDURES

The proportions of tutors 'adjusting' the grades required of candidates to take account of the GCE board which administered the examination, the syllabus examined or the mode of examination were small but markedly different in the three types of institution.

In colleges of further education less than one in twenty tutors recorded that they made such adjustments and board, mode and syllabus were equally likely to be considered as reasons for modifying the required grades. Similar proportions of polytechnic tutors considered that modification of the offer was required in respect of the candidate's board and examination mode but almost one in five adjusted the required grades to take account of the syllabus followed. Approximately half of these tutors took the specific syllabus studied into account when making the initial offer and half were prepared to amend their offer when results were known. One university tutor, clearly upset at the missed opportunity, responded 'I wish we had the information and the resources to do this'. Others were less sure:

Objectively, it is probably desirable to adjust grades to take account of known differences in examining boards at O and A level. However, the basis for doing that is, I think, too insecure. Probably no more harm is done by non-adjustment than might be done through adjusting. (polytechnic, economics)

University tutors adjusting grades to compensate for perceived curricular differences cited particularly syllabuses in engineering, building construction, engineering drawing, general studies, mathematics and statistics, 'mixed' mathematics, modern mathematics, Nuffield physics and SMP mathematics. Polytechnic tutors recorded a similar response in respect of many of these subjects.

Two particular boards were most usually seen as the 'hardest' and a third was most often identified as 'more generous'. No evidence was offered in support of these claims which, nevertheless, were often boldly stated:

board standards vary considerably from subject to subject. (university, law) ... the variable standards of the GCE boards are a concern to us – too little is said of this publicly. (university, history)

Admissions tutors in universities were rather more likely than those in other institutions to adjust grade requirements for these factors. One in twenty modified the grade demanded to take note of the mode of the examination and more than one in ten to counteract the effect of the board. Their main concern was the syllabus of the A-level course followed. The proportion of university tutors claiming that they modified the grade demands for this reason reached one in six. Adjustment was as likely to take place at the time of making the offer as when the results became known.

Tutors in polytechnics and universities held similar views on the importance of a candidate's school or college and a fifth of all tutors adjusted the required grades to account for this when making an offer of a place. A similar proportion were prepared to take this factor into account after the publication of results. One approach was explained:

The department maintains a register of schools in which its own graduates are teachers, or with which the department has special links. Applicants from these schools *may* be treated more favourably on the grounds that we know the teachers and have confidence in their judgement. This is especially the case where such applicants fail to reach the prescribed A-level grades. (university, history)

Others noted:

We are likely to be more lenient in marginal failure for candidates whose school background seems to be disadvantaged. (university, physics)

We would take into account the quality and amount of education received and make allowances for students studying in the evenings, part-time, doing A level in one year or indeed working in difficult circumstances, e.g. non-academic schools, non-academic streams or deprived areas geographically or culturally. (polytechnic, sociology)

If they have studied at a large comprehensive, we are prepared to be more generous and the inverse *may* be true regarding tutorial colleges and the private sector everything else being equal. Also some weight would be given to girls doing non-traditional subjects. (polytechnic, economics)

Using information derived from the UCCA confidential report, similar adjustments were noted by both university and polytechnic tutors for 'inner city schools', schools with 'newly introduced sixth forms' and those 'where teaching staff are inexperienced'. The reverse pattern was also recorded where '... higher standards are expected from certain excellent schools ...' (university, medicine).

SPECIAL COURSE REQUIREMENTS

For admission to two-thirds of the university courses it was essential for candidates to obtain O and A level, and in nine out of ten cases a particular grade was specified as well as a subject. For most other university courses certain subjects were identified as desirable although not essential and this was almost as likely to be applied to O-level subjects as to subjects at A level.

In polytechnics this position was almost exactly replicated although the insistence upon particular subjects applied to rather more of the courses. Almost half the courses also specified grades for required subjects. No demands for named subjects were made by colleges of further education.

Throughout higher education the subjects most often noted as 'essential' at O level were English language and mathematics and, where this was not so, English language alone was the usual requirement. For B.Sc. courses, mathematics and physics were normally seen as essential but, in a few cases, the list once again included English language.

Where this basic O-level core was extended by the addition of 'desirable subjects', these were sometimes the course-related subject also asked for at A level but, more usually, desired subjects were spread across the curriculum including unspecified or specified sciences (usually physics), geography, history and a foreign language. Science courses were rather more likely than arts courses to demand named subjects in addition to the subject-related A-level requirements. Where this occurred, mathematics was the subject most usually included.

In general, admission tutors confirmed published course requirements,* although the returns recorded a slight tendency to increase the course requirements. Thus, English language was often added to a published O-level requirement for mathematics. The differences between published and apparent requirements at A level was usually the addition of a grade to the subject and the new level set was usually B. Whether this revealed 'hidden' requirements or whether course entry requirements had recently been extended was unclear.

Additional entry requirements beyond those already indicated were relatively rarely sought although 'suitability for industrial placement' or 'industrial sponsorship' was a requirement for a few courses. Art and architecture often required the production of a portfolio of work.

THE USE OF ADDITIONAL TESTS FOR ADMISSION

Some form of additional testing of applicants was used by all types of institution although it was nowhere used by the majority. Almost one-third of the further education college courses made some use of tests or essays to assist with their selection. Less than one in fifty of the courses in these

* The *Compendium of University Requirements*, and *The Polytechnic Courses Handbook*, both published annually.

polytechnics and universities expected all candidates to take a test.

The testing of selected applicants was a more common occurrence. Approximately one-third of the polytechnic courses and a sixth of the university courses expected some of their applicants to complete tests or write essays. Most of these were presented to the candidate at or after interview but a few were used to gain additional information before a candidate arrived for interview. In a very few cases the outcomes were used to select for interview.

Less than one in ten of the tests used by further education college tutors involved published material. Approximately one-third used an essay format. In a quarter of the further education courses all candidates were tested although overseas applicants and those lacking formal qualifications were the most likely subjects overall. Two out of three tutors recorded that satisfactory performance in the test was a crucial factor in selection. In other cases tests provided supplementary information or were used to decide upon the level of course to be followed.

Testing in polytechnics was also usually based on departmentally-produced tests or writing an essay, although some use of published tests was made. 'Borderline candidates', 'those about whom we cannot reach a decision', 'dyslexic candidates', 'those without normal qualifications' and 'mature students' were identified as test subjects. The criterion for testing was occasionally related to A-level performance:

Applicants with less than twelve points (A = 3, B = 2, C = 1) are required to take the IBM Programs Attitude Test to indicate whether somewhat borderline candidates have an aptitude for computer studies. (polytechnic, computer science)*

Unqualified and mature students were often asked to write an essay to test, for example:

1 whether they can find the appropriate material in a library;
2 their skill at extracting specific points;
3 the strength of their motivation. (polytechnic, law)

Not all such tests were carried out 'under examination conditions'. Two to three weeks, for example, were allowed for the completion of some essay tests.

Within universities, tests were more likely to be identified as 'for the very few'. Occasional use of published test material was recorded although course-devised 'language' tests were most common. Essays were used to

*The allocation of points in this example does not conform to the more usual pattern described earlier.

'indicate literacy, reasoning and analytical skills'. For a very few courses all those interviewed were tested and for an even smaller group all applicants were tested 'to help assess ability as distinct from ... motivation and effort ...'.

ROLE OF THE ADMISSIONS TUTOR

Many tutors saw their role as a vital one and felt responsibility to both institution and candidate. There were, however, a number of indications that the task of admissions tutor was regarded as a necessary chore for which one was nominated or which one was drafted to undertake. A number of tutors suggested that their fellows within the institution viewed the role in this way and contrasted it with the 'real' tasks of research and teaching.

No example was found of formal training for the task, although an induction period, where duties were shared with the incumbent, was not uncommon. Sometimes the period of overlapping responsibility lasted up to two years, but commonly there was little overlap. Some tutors recorded that they developed their skills 'on the job' and the idea of formal training was rejected in some cases. Tutors, it was explained, 'valued their independence'.* In such circumstances it is not surprising that the need for maturity was stressed by a number who considered that admissions procedures were best left to 'older', 'more experienced', staff.

There were indications that training for the task would not have been amiss in a number of cases. There was, for example, quite a widespread unawareness of the range and meaning of alternative qualifications. (The information provided through SCUE did not, for example appear influential.) Further, interviewing, where it was a feature of selection, was conducted very idiosyncratically and the interview was generally identified as a 'personal' thing. The education sector tended to contrast with industry, where the interview was recognized as a valuable but imperfect tool. It was not clear whether admission tutors were aware of the limitations of the interview as a selection device. One tutor, for example, claimed 'the interview is a good way of recognizing superficiality' (university physics course), and few tutors were critical of their own procedures. A range of factors, including candidate stress, interviewer fatigue and misunderstand-

* W. A. Reid (1974) pointed out that 'admissions tutors do not see themselves as having positions of low autonomy; neither, on the other hand, do they see themselves as "professionals" ... Just as applicants are guided by stereotypes of universities and by the social stabilities of the school ... selectors are guided by the nature and purpose of applicants and of their own departments ... and administrative constraints ...'

ing can make the interview an inaccurate source of information. Training and careful structuring can reduce the difficulties.

Admission to Oxford and Cambridge*

Two major characteristics distinguish admission procedures at Oxford and Cambridge from those used in the remainder of higher and further education: the impact made by the collegiate structure of the two universities and the use made of a specific entrance examination. A third feature, the recruitment of an undergraduate elite, while an undoubted intention might not necessarily distinguish Oxford and Cambridge quite so clearly from the rest of higher education.

While the colleges certainly dominated admission to both universities this was not unchallenged by the subject disciplines. Admissions tutors did, as elsewhere, carry subject roles but they were responsible for selection to all other disciplines as well as their own. The increasing influence being exerted by faculties and departments suggested that the criteria used for admissions had not always provided totally satisfactory undergraduates.

Two positive benefits of the college approach were, however, apparent. The first was the importance attached to the role of admissions tutor. Selection was recognized as a professional and crucial task: it carried status and this helped to sustain a willingness to be involved in the task which was not so clearly evident elsewhere. It also ensured continuity and the development of a professionalism which contrasted quite markedly with the image conveyed by some tutors from other institutions. Admission tutors in other universities and polytechnics seemed generally content to select from those candidates arriving at their institutions. Notwithstanding their atypical situation, Oxford and Cambridge tutors were making very real efforts to increase the number and the diversity of applicants.

The second bonus derived from the continuing personal link between the admissions tutor and the successful applicant. Outside the college system with its routine tutorial meetings, such links, where they did exist, were more distant and tenuous. At Oxford and Cambridge admission tutors co-existed with their mistakes, thus prompting a greater need for certainty at time of admission and also giving rise to a heightened sense of responsibility for subsequent undergraduate success.

The use of an entrance examination also provided a marked contrast with the rest of higher education although, without the forceful pronounce-

* A full description of the admissions procedures at Oxford and Cambridge forms Appendix B.

ments of SCUE, the use of entrance examinations would almost certainly be more widespread. The reaction of a number of admissions tutors elsewhere in higher education to the possible loss of A level as a tool had been to suggest the introduction of a coordinated entrance examination. The modification of S-level papers to serve as a replacement for common entrance papers was also suggested by some tutors at Oxford and Cambridge.

However, while a university-controlled examination solves problems at one level it does give rise to others. While many tutors expressed a reluctance to rely upon A level as the major means of selection, others expressed their doubts about the setting, marking and moderation of common entrance papers. The problem of persuading a wider audience of the fairness of selection by examination was also one which many tutors were aware of. Each university had evolved rather different strategies for the conduct of the entrance examination but neither escaped criticism from inside the university as well as from outside.*

The usefulness of seeing a candidate's unaided work, so often claimed as a major rationale for the continuation of an entrance examination, was an argument that hardly applied at Cambridge. In an attempt to gain objectivity, the tutors had largely been separated from the process of marking the papers of their own applicants.

Conditional offers, widely in use elsewhere, were used by many colleges in both universities. There were, however, differences in their form between Oxford and Cambridge. At Cambridge, conditional offers were set very high, often included specified grades for S-level papers and were aimed at ensuring the recruitment of an elite which had already distinguished itself in public examinations. The number of conditional offers made by some colleges was many times greater than the number of places available. At Oxford, conditional offers allowed a candidate to perform less well on subjects of more marginal importance to the course to be followed. They rarely acknowledged S-level papers and offers were seen as a much firmer indication of a place.

The use of matriculation offers, where a candidate is asked merely to achieve two A-level passes in order to obtain a place, was not encountered

---

* The last months of the Project overlapped the activity of a committee, under the chairmanship of Sir Kenneth Dover, reviewing admissions procedure at Oxford. As a result of the Davis Report, Oxford colleges agreed to abolish the 'seventh term' entrance examination from 1985 for entrants in 1986. The UCCA application form plus a supplementary card will in future serve as the main line of approach to Oxford, with mid-October as the closing date for applications.

outside Oxford and Cambridge. It appeared to be the only remaining use of the original concept of matriculation. While there were clear differences between colleges in the way in which matriculation offers were framed there were no clear patterns which distinguished the two universities. In some colleges it was clear that a small number of matriculation offers were made, largely as a public relations exercise, to demonstrate the wish to recruit students from a variety of backgrounds. Other colleges restricted matriculation offers to those expected to obtain outstanding A-level results. In neither case could the adoption of such practices have other than a marginal effect upon recruitment to higher education as a whole.

Employers and public examinations at 18 +

The general picture with regard to the recruitment of school leavers to industry has been discussed in Chapter II. This section looks again at the selection process, focusing particularly on those aspects which affect candidates at 18 +.

Approximately four in every ten employers indicated that they recruited at 18 +. Although most of this recruitment was to professional and managerial positions – where 18 + qualifications were more than twice as likely to be required by employers as 16 + qualifications – there was clearly some recruitment from the age group to all other categories of employment. Within the category of technical work, 18 + qualifications were featured by over half the employers, but for clerical and sales staff the proportion had fallen to under a half. Within the admittedly much smaller range of qualifications sought for skilled manual and operative posts, 18 + qualifications still featured significantly among the academic requirements listed.

Although the demand for 18 + qualifications was thus largely concentrated in the category of professional and management posts it is probably as important to see this as a function of the age of recruitment to such posts as of the need for applicants to meet specific academic criteria. Overall, most employers saw the interview as marginally more important in selection than qualifications, although relatively few paid as much attention to other factors such as application forms, references or tests. The majority of employers wishing to recruit to professional, managerial and technical posts at 18 +, however, did rank qualifications as more important than the interview.

Six out of ten employers recorded that public examinations were essential to their selection processes, though this opinion was rather more likely to be related to examinations at 16 + than to those at 18 +. Even for professional and managerial posts the proportion claiming that qualifications were essential for selection fell from almost eight in ten with respect to 16 + qualifications, to five in ten for those at 18 +. Consistently, less than half of the employers said they took a rigid line with regard to demands for qualifications.

Employers' requirements from schools and colleges were largely unrelated to the age and experience of the applicant. 'Initiative', 'confidence', 'independence' and 'integrity', however, appeared rather more frequently among the attributes which employers expected applicants to have developed in school by the age of 18.

It was clear that GCE A levels were the 18 + qualifications most commonly required by employers. Thus eight in every ten recruiting for professional and management posts required A levels, about one in five sought BEC awards and rather fewer were looking for TEC qualifications. Within A levels, two or three passes at grade C or better were the most commonly specified, illustrating some overlap between this area of recruitment and selection for higher education. Less than one in five would have been satisfied with an applicant for a professional or managerial post who could offer no more than the pursuit of an A-level course.

Interestingly, employers requiring technicians from this age group were also rather more likely to ask for A-level qualifications than for the seemingly more appropriate awards from the Technician Education Council. When seeking technicians at 18, over half the employers requested A levels, although many more would have been satisfied with applicants who had followed an A-level course rather than obtained specific grades; half sought TEC qualifications and more than one in ten wanted applicants who had followed a CGLI course. Recruitment to clerical and sales appointments at 18 was most likely to be dependent upon RSA and Pitman qualifications although BEC awards were recognized as suitable qualifications by almost a quarter of this group of employers.

In recruitment to the more senior positions, English and mathematics retained their prominence and only in technician recruitment did science displace English in the list of desired subjects. Even for this type of employment technical subjects were preferred only by a minority of employers. It is not clear whether the primacy of English and mathematics reflects a search for general indicators of ability or rather a liking for the familiar and a failure to recognize the relevance of attainment in other subject areas. Such issues require further study before they can be fully explained.

The prestructured questionnaire which was presented to employers could only look superficially at these matters and understanding of the issue was complicated by the overlapping of some of the alternative responses offered. For example, the questionnaire produced over 500 alternative, but non-discrete reasons for requiring academic qualifications from the 149 employers recruiting professional and management personnel.

Seven employers in every ten recruiting at this level affirmed that academic qualifications would be required for subsequent academic courses. Rather fewer recorded that the requirement was determined by the appropriate professional body.

Four out of ten respondents overall saw examinations as a 'measure of intelligence' and a 'predictor of future performance'. A further alternative, which asked whether examination success was 'necessary for successful job performance', received the agreement of almost a third of the total sample.

Overall, four out of ten employers used academic qualifications as a screening device, ensuring that time was not 'wasted' by calling inappropriate candidates to interview. Once again this proportion reached a half for those seeking professional and management recruits at 18 +.

It was difficult to estimate the relative importance accorded to the various aspects of the selection process since, although information concerning the sequence of selection events confirmed an initial reference to an application form by almost all employers, there was no follow-up of the weight given to qualifications at this stage. However, where examination results are used to screen or rank candidates, or where they are a professional or further education requirement, they are likely to be the first matter considered. There can thus be very few professional and management posts which are 'open' to those without evidence of public examination success. If the selection process is the gate to occupation in these positions, examinations are the key which can open the gate.

The subsequent application of non-academic criteria at interview followed a predictable pattern. Aspects such as 'initiative', 'leadership potential', 'appearance' and 'motivation/ambition' were considered relevant to professional and managerial positions by nine in ten employers. 'Academic potential' was required by almost as many employers and more than half were looking for qualities such as 'cooperativeness' 'social acceptability' and 'wide interests' in their potential managers.

Summary and discussion

Public examinations are clearly interwoven with the general processes of assessment in schools, and confusion abounds at 18 +, as at 16 +, concerning their purpose and possibilities. Are they evidence of achievement? Are they a basis for further study? Are they a mechanism for screening and selection? Whatever conclusions are preferred, it is clear that GCE A level is highly prized by many users, and its smaller candidature also sets it apart from its 16 + precursors.

Geographical and socio-economic inequity in the allocation of places in further and higher education seems to have its origins at points well preceding the 18 + selection hurdle. However, the idiosyncratic and irrational basis of much selection appears likely to produce unfairness in individual cases.

Employers made the greatest use of 18 + qualifications in selection for professional and managerial posts, though these had some influence in all categories of employment. As at 16 +, the role of qualifications was largely conditioned by market forces. Certainly such factors were far more influential in determining entry criteria, either to employment or to educational courses, than were the intrinsic challenges of the subsequent activity.

'Grade inflation' tended to lead to university matriculation levels appearing unrealistic and unrelated to the course demands actually made upon students. Many applicants apparently holding appropriate university matriculation requirements had failed in practice to acquire a place on advanced courses in polytechnics or colleges of further education.

The fairly extensive use made of 18 + qualifications to screen out excess applicants for employment also revealed a detachment from educational considerations. Whether pit ponies or dray horses were required only race horses had any chance of success. The way the aggregated points system was used in selection to higher education had little other than administrative convenience to commend it.

Technologically-based qualifications were frequently rejected in favour of almost any A-level success both in education and industry. Much of the use made of A-level results in higher education, particularly in connection with the points system, was inconsistent with traditional concerns for depth rather than breadth in the preparation of candidates. If examination results are to be used in this way then a more broadly based sixth-form curriculum might barely affect selection. Selection conducted along current lines would not guarantee a place for candidates outstanding in their fields of interest unless they also excelled in other disciplines. In industry, for example in recruitment to technician posts where specific vocationally-oriented qualifications fared badly in comparison to A level, the same process could be seen at work. Employers did not, of course, control the conditions attached to professional membership and it is possible that some of these entry requirements need reassessing.

Admissions tutors had remarkable autonomy and demonstrated very different levels of understanding and competence. Outside Oxford and Cambridge, where the admissions role was prized and offered high status, tutors' obligations competed heavily with the demands of teaching and research. The continuing close link between admissions tutor and successful applicant to Oxford and Cambridge also brought a greater sense of personal responsibility into the selection procedure. Selectors often defended their claim to be allowed to act without interference, and rejected the idea of training for the post.

Variables associated with examination board, syllabus and mode of examination were not used extensively as discriminating features in selection although in some cases this was due to a lack of information rather than to any acceptance of comparability. There were a few signs that a mythology of board and mode differences was being perpetuated.

Specific entrance hurdles, exemplified by testing in some colleges of further education and by employers – and also by Oxford and Cambridge entrance examinations – were not self-evident improvements to the process of selection. It can be argued that while such assessments cannot be as sophisticated as professionally prepared public examinations (a view supported by many within Oxbridge), they can focus upon crucial aspects of performance in a way that no 'general purpose' examination can. However, it remains true that entry to Oxford and Cambridge is perceived as inequitable by many outside and not a few inside the system. It may indeed prove impossible to persuade the wider public otherwise without radical change.

IV. Users' views of examinations and some alternatives

Examinations at 16+ and 18+ are mechanisms allowing candidates to demonstrate what they have achieved. But where certificates are likely to be used by others it is obviously important to describe performance in ways which take cognizance of users' views. This chapter explores those features of examinations which users currently find helpful and those which appear to create difficulties. It also looks at users' reactions to a number of alternative approaches to documenting achievement.

Knowledge of the system of examinations

Almost three-quarters of the employers considered that they knew 'sufficient' about the present system of examinations and a further fifth claimed that they knew 'a lot'. However, J. A. B. Baird (1981) explored Manchester employers' knowledge of GCE and CSE examinations and, while more than half of these claimed to be familiar with the field, only 3 per cent were able to answer correctly four fundamental questions on the present system.

A quarter of the companies in Baird's survey 'were wholly committed to the GCE system', more than a third saw an average pupil as one who 'was capable of O-level grade C or better', and CSE Mode III examinations were 'a mystery' to four in every five. He concluded that not only were candidates offering CSE qualifications likely to be discriminated against but that rejection was likely to extend to candidates offering O level passes at lower grades since these were also seen as 'failures'. Baird allocated responsibility for this flood of misinformation evenly: schools had failed to inform on curriculum and grouping practices; examination boards had failed to inform on the meaning of examination results; and employers had failed to seek that information which was available or to consider the implications of particular levels of performance for their own occupations. E. S. Freedman (1979) and E. Reid (1980) each offer confirmation for some of Baird's conclusions.

In the light of these findings it is likely that the seemingly satisfactory picture of employers' understanding arising in the present study should be treated with caution. In general, the few employers who reported that their knowledge of the system was insufficient underlined the point with comments confirming this lack of knowledge or with enquiries about the system of grading currently in use. Others wanted to know more about 'optional and compulsory subjects'.

The knowledge of the system displayed by educational users of examinations was not always convincing. Many admissions tutors, for example, were unaware of official equivalences between examinations. Those who had discovered the objectives and content of different syllabuses or explored the implications of mode and title differences were very rare. Predictions of student success did not generally reflect specific consideration of such factors, though some users from the educational sector raised more philosophical issues:

Fundamentally I question what Os and As test and the purposes to which they are put. I'm deeply concerned by the way the country controls employment on the basis of a test so heavily biased towards facts of memory [O levels] and universities base their entrance requirements on an exam which is a poor predictor of university performance ... various professions use both exams though no one seems to know what these exams really test (other than the ability to pass exams). Surely we desperately need tests of initiative, energy, dynamism etc? (girls' independent school)

A number of questions involve the plethora of examinations that have cropped up over the years and therefore the point of recognition of awards. Even on the matter of entry to BEC National course, there are variations of interpretation of awards and qualifications. Some centres, for example, insist on passes in English language and maths for BEC National students, although this is not specifically required by BEC. Perhaps the most important issue raised is the nature and purpose (educational, social and even economic!) of assessment and the recognition of awards. (further education college, non-advanced course)

The present system of examining at 16 +

This section includes the views of educational users of GCE O level and CSE from all types of provision. Across the whole range a remarkably constant 90 per cent provided their opinions. Employers' views have been incorporated wherever possible though their much lower response rate and tendency to submit incomplete questionnaires has meant that the information is less reliable.

GCE O LEVEL
Maintenance of certification
A clear majority of those from all sectors of education considered that the present system of recording O-level examination performance should be maintained.

Those who gave no opinion on the perpetuation of the present O-level certification were always in the minority so, perhaps inevitably, familiarity or involvement tended to give rise to either agreement or disagreement rather than indifference. Within schools and among tutors providing GCE courses elsewhere, those giving no opinion formed approximately 5 per cent of the sample. This figure rose to almost 20 per cent among tutors of advanced courses in further education colleges and polytechnics. The extremes of opinion on the question of changing the form of O-level reporting were represented by university tutors, less than one in ten of whom thought that the system should be changed, and GCE A-level course tutors in all sectors (a good proportion of whom were also inevitably teaching O-level courses) where a fifth felt that change was needed.

When the position in the school sector was looked at more closely it became clear that teachers supporting change were most likely to be employed in comprehensive schools and sixth-form colleges, where the full range of ability was likely to be encountered. Those favouring the maintenance of O level were proportionately more common in grammar schools, and to a slightly lesser degree in independent schools.

A majority of employers across all types of employment were satisfied with the information about an applicant's attainment and potential conveyed by the examination result. Those recruiting to technical posts were most likely to feel that the examination certificate had provided them with adequate information. However, the proportion of employers who were dissatisfied with the information provided on current certificates was consistently a third of those responding from all types of employment.

Grading
The present GCE O-level certificate offers five grades ranging from A to E with a final 'unclassified' category. Most respondents expressed an opinion about the number of grades currently used in the O-level examination although the proportion not expressing a view increased with 'distance' from the examination, rising to one in five among tutors in colleges of further education, polytechnics and universities. Throughout all types of provision the majority view was that there were currently neither too many nor too few grades. These opinions were strongly endorsed within schools

and sixth-form colleges, where they were supported by eight in every ten teachers, and offered least support in further education colleges. Independent and grammar schools differed from the remainder of the maintained sector in respect of the proposition that O level offered too few grades. Teachers from these two types of school, while still remaining in a minority, were twice as likely to agree with this proposition as were teachers elsewhere. The 'new' system of recording O-level results was still an issue for many users:

The new system of recording O-level results is confusing. Grades A to C are passes. Grades D and E are fails and do not deserve certification. I would prefer to revert to the old method. (girls' comprehensive school)

The prospect of recording results by means of pass/fail grades was uniformly rejected by nine in ten of those working in all types of institution and was an issue about which very few remained indifferent.

Extending the range of information included
The inclusion of syllabus descriptions on O-level certificates was an issue about which no consensus was apparent. In many institutions respondents were almost equally divided between agreeing, disagreeing, and having no opinion on this possibility. O-level syllabus descriptions were seen as almost irrelevant by the time candidates had reached university, but even in schools and further education colleges under half of those providing A-level courses (where it might be assumed that such material would be most useful), agreed that details of syllabus should be included. In sixth form colleges, where students from a variety of school backgrounds have to be quickly assimilated, more than seven in ten teachers agreed with the inclusion of syllabus information on the O-level certificate.

The position concerning the provision of graded information or profiling grades, showing attainment in different aspects of subject, was much more clear-cut. Although up to one-third of the respondents had no opinion, over half of the respondents in all institutions disagreed with the inclusion of such information. The strong rejection of this proposition was particularly interesting in the light of work currently taking place in a number of examination boards (notably the Associated Examining Board, the Joint Matriculation Board, the Oxford Delegacy of Local Examinations and University of London School Examination Department) to determine the feasibility of providing just this type of information.* Two sixth-form

* See also Harrison, 1983.

tutors in comprehensive schools provided examples of the width of the divide over this issue:

I would like [O-level] certificates to show separate paper scores, e.g. multiple-choice, short answer, essay questions. I can't think why the boards won't provide this unless it is for their own protection.

The certificate would become too complicated... It would require a lot of study... to actually see what it meant...

Views on whether O-level certificates should carry an indication of how the candidate's grade related to the achievement of all pupils in that age group were also inconsistent and showed considerable variation between the different types of provision. In school sixth forms and non-advanced further education college courses (including GCE), respondents were rather more likely to disagree with this suggestion than to agree with it. The balance was a fairly fine one with up to one in five tutors not expressing a strong opinion on the matter. Tutors for advanced further education college courses and those working in polytechnics and universities were rather more likely to support the proposition than disagree with it, but in these sectors the proportion of respondents unable to express a clear opinion increased to three and even four in every ten.

Small differences of opinion were noted between the different types of school with regard to extending the range of information provided on O-level certificates. As with other propositions, teachers in independent and grammar schools were rather more likely to support the status quo than teachers in other schools. Thus more than six in ten teachers in these two types of school disagreed with providing an indication of differential performance within a subject and with showing the skills and knowledge associated with a given grade.

Pupil profiles

In the light of opinions concerning the maintenance of the present O-level certificates, it was hardly surprising to note that the replacement of GCE O levels by a system of achievement profiles – recording academic attainment, personal qualities and interests – was overwhelmingly rejected. The proportion of those rejecting the proposal was never less than three-quarters of respondents in all types of institution.

A pupil profile to supplement the information available on the O-level certificate did, however, receive the approval of a majority. A supplementary profile gained most support in schools, where seven out of ten teachers endorsed it, whereas within universities and polytechnics the issue was rendered less clear with a quarter of the tutors recording that they had no opinion on the issue. Supplementary profiles were rejected by a rather higher proportion of teachers in independent and grammar schools than by teachers in other types of school. Two examples capture some of the fundamental issues of profiling:

I would like to see some form of profile at 16 + and 18 + *incorporating* examination results (as a form of moderation of the profile). In this format I would see comments on pupils' attainments in different aspects of a subject (rather than grades) as valuable. I would prefer neither exam certificate nor profile to be used separately. (boys' comprehensive school)

I am concerned at the present drive for 'student profiles'. They seem to me to be no more useful than a normal reference and would not therefore help in the employment field. Within the schools they would become either an administrative chore for busy form tutors or would be used as a 'carrot' and would have all the subjective pressures on form tutor and student of the need to praise in order to reward improvement. (girls' comprehensive school)

The rather problematic issue of profiles has been explored extensively elsewhere and similar differences of opinion documented among those using pupil profiles (Balogh, 1982; DES, 1983) and those developing them (Goacher, 1983a).

Employers produced a somewhat ambiguous response to the idea of a profile of academic and non-academic information. Some, who supported the idea, pointed to the need for (at least) local standardization as well as to the importance of avoiding bias. While a few unreservedly welcomed any system which better organized the information appropriate to selection, more commonly there were doubts:

Do most teachers have enough information about their pupils to make profiles worthwhile? Profiles should give an actual, not an idealistic, picture of the pupil. Before completing profiles teachers need a wider appreciation of the career opportunities available to their pupils and should adopt an unprejudiced view of industry and commerce. (employer supporting the principle of pupil profiles)

Those who rejected the idea saw a danger of stereotyping and appreciated the need to leave the referee to express himself or herself freely, admitting that they disliked the limitations imposed by standardized forms. Some explained that confidential information was best obtained by telephone and a few made it clear that any references were only taken up after an appointment had been made, apparently unaware of the strength of feeling which exists in educational circles concerning the unprofessional nature of this practice.

CSE

Maintenance of certification

The general view within schools and among tutors of advanced and non-advanced courses in further education colleges and polytechnics was in favour of retaining the present system of recording CSE examination performance, although the majority was not always a large one. Quite large proportions also registered no opinion, about a third of the advanced course tutors and polytechnic lecturers, for example. Opinion among GCE course tutors in colleges of further education was almost equally divided between agreeing, disagreeing and having no opinion on the retention of the CSE system of recording performances.

The perceived irrelevance of the CSE examination to many university tutors was underlined by the fact that more than half of them recorded 'no opinion' on the matter. The same pattern of response was repeated for all other questions concerned primarily with the CSE examination: less than half, and sometimes as few as a third, of university tutors expressed an opinion. Only within schools did the maintenance of CSE certification receive clear-cut support, with seven in ten of teachers agreeing that it should be maintained. However, even in the school sector a sixth of the teachers disagreed with its continuation, and the amount of support the examination received varied with the type of school.

The majority in favour of retaining the examination was largest in comprehensive schools where more than seven in ten teachers agreed with its retention. In grammar schools and sixth form colleges this proportion fell to six in ten and in independent schools there was a fairly even balance between teachers supporting retention and those registering 'no opinion' on the survival of CSE certification.

Grading

CSE results are graded on a scale from 1 to 5 with an unclassified category for performances below grade 5. Very few users of the examinations either considered that this pattern of grading offered too few alternatives or indicated that they wished to decrease the number of grades. Among the tutors of non-advanced further education courses, however, there were indications of a substantial body of opinion in favour of reducing the number of CSE grades to three or four, this alternative being supported by slightly less than half the respondents.

Not unexpectedly there was little support for the introduction of a pass/fail grading system in the examination. Indeed, even within universities a majority of respondents rejected this proposal, perhaps indicating a general disenchantment with this form of recording achievement. Pass/fail grading was rejected by nine out of ten teachers, by eight out of ten tutors in further education colleges and polytechnics, and by seven out of ten university lecturers.

There was little disparity of view between the different types of school concerning alternative CSE grading patterns.

*Extending the range of information included**

While in all sectors those supporting an extension of the information included on the CSE certificate outnumbered those opposed to the idea, only among tutors of non-advanced further education courses was there a clear majority in favour.

The recording on the CSE certificate of the skills and knowledge which a pupil had acquired was rejected by a majority of respondents from all sectors of education. Nor was the inclusion on the certificate of a profile of different aspects of a candidate's performance supported in any sector by more than a quarter of respondents.

Users, from all types of provision other than universities were very evenly divided over the issue of providing an indication of how the candidate's performance compared with the achievement of all pupils in the age group. Approximately one-third approved of giving some indication, one-third opposed it and one-third expressed no opinion. Over half the university tutors recorded that they had no opinion on the matter.

Nor was the provision of more detailed information on the CSE certificate an issue which gave rise to great differences of view in the different types of school. Apart from the position of sixth-form college tutors, referred to in connection with O level, the only variation was in the rather greater proportion of teachers in independent and grammar schools who indicated that they had no opinion on the matter.

Pupil profiles

Six out of ten respondents rejected any replacement of the CSE certificate by a pupil profile. Within schools and colleges of further education there was a clear overall majority, however, in favour of supplementing the information provided by a CSE certificate with a pupil profile recording academic achievements, personal qualities and interests. This majority was largest among sixth-form college and comprehensive school staff and only in independent schools did rather more teachers record 'no opinion' than

* A number of CSE boards already offer descriptions of the performance levels implied by particular grades.

agree with such a supplement. In polytechnics and universities the division of opinion was more finely balanced with as many as four in ten tutors having no opinion on the proposal although, even in these institutions, over a third of the respondents approved of the suggestion.

CONTRASTING PERCEPTIONS OF GCE O LEVEL AND CSE
In all sectors of education the proportion of respondents agreeing with the maintenance of the O-level examination was considerably larger than those offering support to CSE. The difference between the two was at its lowest within schools and reached a maximum in the universities. These differential responses to O level and CSE should perhaps be seen as a clear refutation of the old adage that distance lends enchantment, for certainly those in higher education saw CSE certification as peripheral to their requirements.

There were only minor differences of opinion about the propositions that CSE and GCE certificates included too large a range of grades and any differences concerning pass/fail grades were swamped by overall disapproval of this approach. There were, however, clear distinctions in response to the suggestion that O-level and CSE certificates provided too few grades. Thus, although few respondents considered that this was true of CSE, the proportion considering that O level had too few alternatives varied between 6 per cent in schools and 20 per cent in sixth form colleges. It must be remembered that while O-level and CSE certificates offer an identical number of grades, the range of attainment represented by a single grade is very different for the two examinations, with CSE grades tending to cover broader spreads of achievement.

Opinions concerning the merit of providing details of syllabus, performance and the candidate's normative placement hardly varied between O level and CSE. Nor did opinions concerning the use of a supplementary profile differentiate between the two examinations. Perhaps most surprisingly, the somewhat contentious issue of replacing either examination by a profile brought about an equal, albeit opposed, expression of opinion.

Where respondents made additional comment they often attacked the 'poor self-image of CSE candidates', their 'poor performance' and the examination's 'variable standards between schools'. 'CSE 1 does *not* equal O-level grade C' was a commonly expressed (if inaccurately phrased) judgement.

Criticism of the present system of examinations from employers indicated there was no consensus concerning what was wrong or what might be done to put it right. Thus, while some criticized (inaccurately) the 'continuous assessment of the CSE examination because it does not predict subsequent performance', many others recorded that they would prefer 'more continuous assessment throughout [the] school career than dependence upon one set of examinations'. Some felt that everything that was provided at present had little value: 'Examination results are relatively meaningless but general [school] references contain far too little information'.

Some employers displayed a lack of consistency in their answers. One, for example, who had recorded that public examinations were an essential factor in selection, later made the observation: 'Ability to pass examinations [gives] no indication of ability – we have had to dismiss graduates who were totally unsuited to commercial life'.

There was evidence of strong anti-CSE views among respondents from all sectors of education and by many employers. While some provided considered arguments for their ideas, the factual inaccuracies of others suggested their views to be largely rooted in prejudice. Many of the opinions appeared to be based upon the premise that all pupils should be able to 'pass' O-level examinations. Other common misconceptions were that CSE certificates were obtained by continuous assessment alone with no examined component and that CSE examinations were set, marked and validated entirely within the candidate's school. Such views were not limited to employers but appeared also to have reasonable currency within further and higher education. Some at least realized their lack of knowledge: 'I think O level is a bad exam but I do not know enough about the CSE and other alternatives.' (polytechnic, English)

THE FUTURE OF 16+ EXAMINING

This section concentrates on the views of employers and selectors in further and higher education, although many schools were eager to express their opinions:

A 16 + examination is urgently needed. The examination period in fifth year as it extends from February to June seems to be wasteful of teacher-time. It is felt that all certificates should contain results of a standardized graded test in literacy and numeracy. (comprehensive school)

O level suits boys in my school but nationally I would be in favour of a common system of examining. Surely O and CSE is as divisive as Grammar and Secondary Modern? (boys' independent school)

I feel that a common examination at 16 + is essential and that the number of boards should be reduced. Schools should have to enter pupils for the examinations of their own area board. (comprehensive school)

The present examination system compartmentalizes knowledge and skills to such an extent that both teacher and taught live in an unreal, inflexible limbo that has little relevance to a rapidly changing world. With the traditional justification – 'pass exams and you'll get a job' – for everybody to play along quietly with an outmoded system fast disappearing, teachers will soon find themselves unable to control children, unless we produce new ideas over the next few years ... I know limbo cannot be flexible or inflexible but I feel strongly! I have to add that because some things done at school are examined, many other things learnt and skills acquired are regarded as inferior because they are not examined and graded by an external board. (mixed independent school)

Increasingly I am coming to the conclusion that our exam system is archaic and destructive. It is a system essentially designed to create failure, it totally dominates our education system and not only is it unsound in practice but in theory too. It benefits the few at the expense of the many. 16 + reform and profiles, and especially teacher assessments, show the way forward. (comprehensive school)

The view from further education
Within colleges of further education a quarter of the tutors unreservedly approved of the proposals to restructure examinations at 16 +. When those expressing some reservations about the organization of a new examination were added, the proportion approving the idea in principle rose to one-third.

Tutors from GCE and other non-advanced courses were rather more likely to support the proposal, up to two-fifths of them approving the change in principle.

Comments supportive of change were often couched in phrases such as: 'Any system which rationalizes the present proliferation of examinations would be worthy of consideration'. Other tutors identified possible advantages for their students:

The system of school streaming is in my opinion unfair to students' progress. Many students who make excellent progress at college often come to us very deflated having been initially streamed into CSE courses at school, made to feel inferior, thus eroding their ambition.

Reservations were most commonly phrased in terms of the necessity of maintaining current standards. A typical comment of this type suggested:

[A common examination at 16 +] would be very satisfactory provided that the educational attainment of students is maintained at the present level and the system of recording this level of attainment can be easily compared with past standards.

Some of the reservations, however, originated from a more fundamental critique of the examination system:

Although good in concept, [the common examination at 16 +] would appear in the way it is being approached to:
a perpetuate uncritically a subject-based system
b disadvantage those below the 60th percentile.

Practical considerations caused others to have doubts:

In principle this is a good idea but from my very limited experience of this type of exam I feel that the difficulty lies in the wording of the questions and arranging the contents of the paper to suit the wide ability range of pupils who will be taking this type of exam.

Almost one in four tutors of advanced further education courses (a greater proportion than in any other group) strongly disapproved of proposals for merging CSE and GCE.

Sixteen plus – rubbish. Examinations and syllabus content are interlinked. At the age of sixteen the britest [sic] students must be studying material and answering questions which are entirely different from the weakest students.

I strongly oppose this. We have destroyed so much of our educational heritage over the past two decades. Let's maintain this one remaining differential ... I have great faith in our present examination system and deplore any prospect of change, which I feel will be for the worse.

Strong objections to the planned modifications were expressed by little more than one in ten tutors overall and were often expressed in rather general terms: 'As retrograde as most other so-called reforms in recent years'. Responsibility for the need to maintain the present system was often placed by tutors upon users: 'Disagree with the proposal if only because this is yet another change, employers are confused enough!' A rather larger group expressed doubts about the feasibility of the proposal and the usefulness of the subsequent examination to either candidates or users.

Questions about changing the system of examinations at 16 + often produced a defence of external examinations from tutors, for example:

Whatever the faults of public examinations they represent the best system available. With internally assessed examinations teachers could come under great pressure from pupils/parents to record only satisfactory results. Again, externally set examinations are a safeguard against teachers under pressure falling into the temptations (a) to teach only what they know to be on the examination papers, and (b) to avoid keeping up to date.

The view from higher education
Perhaps because of the perceived irrelevance of examinations at 16 + to

many of those working in higher education, this sector provided little evidence of strong approval or disapproval of possible change. One in five approved the idea of change without reservation and only one in twenty expressed outright disapproval. Where disapproval was expressed, however, it was in strong terms:

Reform is one of the more stupid ideas of recent years . . . . O and A (levels) should in no circumstances be phased out . . . Although actual proof may be lacking . . . any lecturer is aware of students being less well prepared, less well motivated and less good than fifteen years ago . . . The present exam format has worked well for a long time . . . it would seem sensible for bodies such as the Schools Council to stop meddling until something better is found. (university, mathematics)

While a number of university tutors recorded their doubts and fears about the possible consequences of such an introduction, a 16 + examination was not seen in anything like such problematic terms by polytechnic lecturers and almost a third of these unreservedly welcomed the proposals.

Any simplification would be desirable. The argument that they are non-comparable groups educationally is irrelevant as, whether we like it or not, comparison must be made. I would like to see fewer exam boards and a greater standardization of syllabuses between those that remain. (polytechnic, economics)

The view from industry
Approximately half of the employers recorded their approval of the status quo, yet almost four in ten considered that a single examination system at 16 + was desirable. This support was sometimes expressed in terms of a need for a 'national examination board' but more often the plea was for a single, uniform grading system. A large number of employers placed this and a request for more information about the content of syllabuses as their top priorities. Less than one in a hundred considered that examinations at 16 + should be discontinued. The major consideration for employers appeared to be a concern to retain examinations with which they were familiar, although as has already been suggested, many of them had only a superficial understanding of the present system.

The present system of examining at 18 +

This section concentrates on the views of advanced course tutors in further education colleges and lecturers in polytechnics and universities. No common attitude to examining at 18 + was apparent among employers although their interests were sometimes considered by other users:

The only reason for an A-level course, plus subsequent assessment, which can possibly 'hold water' at present is that universities and polytechnics require students to have studied successfully to a certain minimum academic level. Employers using A-level criteria do so at their peril, except in so far as they themselves will require employees to continue their studies as part of their jobs (e.g. banks, libraries, technician appointments). (polytechnic, physics)

GCE A LEVEL

Maintenance of certification
In no type of educational institution did the proportion of respondents supporting the phasing out of public examinations at 18+ exceed 1 per cent. The vast majority also agreed with the retention of A level in its present form. With less than one in ten holding no opinion and a similar proportion recording opinions favouring some reform, the opposition to the most recent attempt to change the structure of A level was confirmed. As with the collation of information on the N and F debate (Schools Council, 1980a), it was clear that although a majority of respondents rejected proposals for change 'the opposition arose from a variety of beliefs'.* In the current study nine in every ten admissions tutors favoured the retention of A level in its present form.

In those few cases where support for reform was indicated, the suggestions made were most commonly concerned with 'broadening the syllabus' although a few tutors also felt that more recognition should be given to those currently 'just failing' A level.

Grading
Pass/fail was rejected by a clear majority of tutors, as it had been in respect of grading performances at 16 +. Similarly, few tutors felt that the number of alternative gradings available at 18 + was too small, although up to a quarter recorded no opinion at this level. There were, however, institutional differences in respect of the proposition that A level offered too many grades. A quarter of advanced course tutors in further education colleges felt that there were currently too many A-level grades whereas less than one in ten of university tutors agreed. Such disparity in views can perhaps be attributed to the rather more selective approach necessary in universities. Some confirmation for this was offered by the intermediate position of polytechnic lecturers. Despite these differences a majority of

* The major beliefs documented in that study were: satisfaction with the present system; preference for gradual change; opposition to external examinations; desire for more radical change; identification of alternative priorities and concern over educational standards.

respondents from all types of institution considered that the number of A-level grades was not too large.

The providers of A-level courses were not always quite so certain of the value or the structure of the existing system:

At A level – magical qualities are attributed to a grade B or C or D which may be marginal differences out of three papers. While some selectors are sensitive, others are not. (comprehensive school)

Extending the information provided on certificates
Extending the information provided on the A-level certificate was not a subject which gave rise to strong expressions of opinion from either further or higher education. Indeed the largest group of respondents, occasionally reaching 50 per cent, were those offering no opinions at all. With the notable exception of those recruiting to language courses in higher education (e.g. French, linguistics) – where an overwhelming majority favoured the inclusion of separate grades showing attainment in different aspects of the subject at A level – there was little strength of feeling about the provision of more details about an A-level candidate's syllabus, performance, knowledge, skill or normative placement.

Pupil profiles
More than eight in ten tutors disagreed with the proposition that A-level certificates could be replaced by a pupil profile. Within universities the proportion was even higher. There was, however, majority support among further education college and polytechnic tutors for the introduction of a profile to supplement the A-level certificate. Among university tutors the largest group agreed but this did not represent a clear majority.

The timing of results
In view of the crucial place of A-level results in determining the final number of students attending a course in higher education, it was surprising that substantial numbers of admission tutors expressed no opinion on the timing of results. Those who recorded their views were, in a proportion of two to one, in favour of an earlier publication of results and this was a suggestion also made by a small number of employers.

THE FUTURE OF 18 + EXAMINING
Current proposals to reform examinations at 18 + concentrate upon the introduction of an intermediate (I-level) examination* between GCE O

---
* I level, recommended in Schools Council (1980b), was also featured in *Examinations 16–18* (DES, 1980b).

and A levels. While no specific information was collected in respect of I level, a number of respondents – in describing the 'problems of A level' – suggested where reform was required:

For languages it is necessary to reform many of the syllabus options offered by the boards. Literature, particularly of the 17th and 18th century schools, is hardly suitable for 17-year-olds. Many of the themes in the texts chosen are beyond the personal experience and even the imagination of young people of this age. (polytechnic, modern languages)

The greatest problem is the unsuitability of A-level studies as a general indicator of academic ability and suitability for higher education. ... This is clearly related to the inter-disciplinary nature of computer studes, whose A levels are still poorly developed and perhaps still inadequate. I am always looking for a breadth of skills and an intellectual liveliness which is apparently rarely fostered in traditional A-level courses, and I very much regret student choices of mixed subjects at A levels becoming even more difficult. The maths/physics/chemistry and the English/history/geography streams are not helpful to my subject. (polytechnic, computer science)

An examination system that merely assesses with a final paper cannot satisfactorily reveal what a pupil *does* know or what kind of person he is. It also fails to take account of pressures that affect the person and colour the nature of the learning. Even at A level the two-year span with a final detailed revision of all material is inappropriate and does not provide the best motivation. It would be better to have a series of detailed internal modules, followed by a final paper on the lines of the special paper where learning could be drawn together in more general terms. (comprehensive school)

The basic intention behind the N and F proposals, to encourage a broader base of secondary education, was a sound one and with more skilful and sensitive advocacy they ought in the end to be able to commend the degree of respect that they require. If, however, they were [to be] introduced in the teeth of vigorous opposition, the whole process could undermine confidence in the system of public examinations, which would be a disaster. (university, education)

Summary and discussion

In general, most respondents were critical of the present system of examinations but there appeared to be a need to perceive a direct personal benefit before any change would be contemplated. Those selecting for sixth-form courses were, for example, almost alone in favouring the provision of more detailed information on O-level certificates. The lack of interest in anything related to CSE on the part of those in universities represented a rather depressing example of this distancing.

This sort of approval must raise suspicion that detailed profiles would be neglected, not because the information would be of little value but because the system would increase the users' administrative load. Such an interpretation would also explain the somewhat illogical support given to the idea of increasing the graded divisions of O level, where the range of performance allocated to each grade is narrow, while a similar suggestion was rejected in respect of CSE, where the performance range within each grade is much wider. Finer grading at O level was seen as potentially useful in the screening of applicants. The broader range of performance within each CSE grade was considered of minimal assistance because the examination itself was dismissed as irrelevant in many settings.

Only among those working in colleges of further education was the information conveyed by CSE certification seen as valuable and therefore in need of a more detailed approach.

Users were often ill-informed and sometimes prejudiced. For selectors in the educational sector in particular it was difficult to offer excuses for ignorance of well-established systems. While examination boards are large and powerful enough to survive misconceptions and ill-informed criticism, the same cannot be said of individual candidates. Candidates are vulnerable and susceptible to long-term damage. If certification conveys primarily disadvantage the system will, in turn, suffer the consequence.

Educational selectors, particularly in higher education, have room to develop more acceptable selection criteria and more professional ways of working. In the interests of equity and openness their autonomy and their judgements should reasonably be subject to scrutiny.

At 18 + only the needs of those continuing directly further to higher education appeared to merit attention from many respondents. The use made of A-level results, already detailed in Chapter III, explains all too clearly why few selectors for higher education pressed the case for more detailed information or indeed for reform.

Thus, while there appeared to be wide support for the status quo at both 16 + and 18 +, particularly in respect of GCE, it was clear that this did not rest upon a firm basis of agreement. There were many shared misunderstandings of the objectives, practices and target populations of current public examinations and these contributed more than a little to the strong arguments that nothing which would meet the range of different objections could be found.

V. Implications for the Future

J. Roach (1971) in his historical overview, makes a point that remains valid:

Examinations can by their nature be nothing more than tools, the means of attaining certain objectives external to themselves. The real interest of the story, both in administrative reform and in education, is in the problem of why at a particular moment in time these tools should have appeared to so many people to be a useful way of achieving certain desirable goals.

This study has, however, made clear that a continuing confusion exists about the fundamental purposes of public examinations. Are examinations at 16 + a culmination of eleven years of compulsory education or a bridge between education or employment? Can they fulfil these quite discrete functions with any degree of efficiency? Are examinations at 18 + a validation of two further years of education or a selection device for higher education? The research has shown that whereas some users seek alternative insights into an applicant's potential, others are satisfied to accept an examination result as the ultimate arbiter. Examinations are often imbued with the powers of 'maintaining standards' and 'objectivity', and their processes – including preparation, conduct and certification – are surrounded with a quite remarkable mystique.

A preoccupation with examinations has been called 'mistaking the shadow for the substance',* but there can be little question that public examinations are inextricably linked to the processes of teaching and learning in the secondary school. What examinations measure is closely tied to a range, albeit narrow, of valued educational outcomes, though the 16 + and 18 + systems have rather different impacts on teaching and learning.

History suggests that examinations, like so many other British traditions, are reformed only at times of crisis. Many examination issues – the diversity of provision, the impact made and the means of control – are relatively unchanging. There are other constant concerns such as what examinations

---

*Peter Andrews. Address to South Eastern Area Secondary Heads Association Conference, 25th January, 1983.

measure, how results are recorded, how consistently and accurately assessment can be carried out and the relationship between examination systems. The current high level of interest in the effects and effectiveness of public examinations may therefore relate to social and economic factors as much as to educational process and product.

There is doubtless a lack of confidence in examinations in some quarters. But if, for example, it is an uncertain relationship between attainment – as measured by examination success – and employability which is the cause of current questioning, then much caution will be required before embarking on any programme of major reform. The relationship between educational attainment and occupational success has never been a simple causal one (see, for example, Hickox, 1983). Certainly, there is no evidence to indicate that unemployment is created by a lack of examination qualifications, a failure to give due weight to basic skills or to any other curriculum imbalance. The current high level of unemployment masks relationships between qualifications and progress, but it would be naive to assume that examination reform can resolve major but non-contingent social problems.

Thus far this report has explored the use made of public examinations at 16 + and 18 + and has given an account of the views and opinions of users. It has illustrated the confusion about examinations and their uses which exists at both major selection points. While the research did not seek the views of the general public, further confusion might reasonably be assumed. If some of those directly concerned in the provision and use of examinations have so little understanding of the system then those outside the fold have little chance indeed.

This chapter will reconsider a number of issues which need to be addressed by both providers and users of examinations and will offer an agenda for those wishing to review the system.

A review of some issues

Research of this kind cannot offer definitive statements of views, attitudes and actions upon which to base future policy. It can, however, provide insights into what is done and into the beliefs which underpin practice although, even here, there is no clear relationship between the strength of feelings expressed by respondents and the importance of any particular issue.

SHOULD PUBLIC EXAMINATIONS BE ABOLISHED

This study did not reveal much enthusiasm for the abolition of examinations. Examinations make a major contribution to the occupational life of most of those questioned whether in schools, colleges, industry or commerce and it is not surprising to find in each sector considerable support for the status quo. Whether a broader sample of those employed at the chalkface and on the workshop floor would replicate this view is open to question.

Certainly, examinations have been under attack from many quarters. The former Chief Inspector of Schools has said that there are too many examinations and that they are too influential.* HM Inspectorate has identified an over-emphasis on 16+ examinations which restricts the opportunities of even academically able students (see, for example, DES, 1979a or, for the application of the critique to a particular school, the HMI report on Chelmsford High School, 1983). Examinations have been accused of providing inaccurate estimates of ability since they measure limited academic objectives (e.g. Burgess and Adams, 1980), and of obstructing the creation of a society able to respond to changing circumstances (e.g. Flude and Parrott, 1979). There have been calls for the replacement of examinations by pupil profiles of achievement (e.g. Mansell, 1982) as well as renewed attacks upon the expenditure of a larger proportion of the shrinking education budget upon examinations – especially those at 16+.

It can be argued that those who support the dismantling of the system ignore reality. Certainly one must recognize that public examinations have been, for many years, the major mechanism for achieving some national control of the secondary curriculum. The reincarnation of a Secondary Examinations Council confirms that the use of such a mechanism will not readily be given up. There also seem, at present, to be a number of obstacles in the way of achieving a national record of achievement sufficiently acceptable to replace or supplement examination results (e.g. Goacher, 1983a).

This research has, however, indicated that examinations have been devalued in practice by users and that they are often being used in an arbitrary and insensitive way at the entrance to sixth-form courses and at admission to further and higher education and to employment. There is a need to restore confidence by clarifying what examinations can satisfactorily measure and by ensuring that the results of examinations are used sensibly and sensitively. If we are to avoid Skilbeck's (1983) prophecy of 'increasing entropy (disorder) leading to the ultimate collapse of the sys-

* Address to Secondary Heads Association, quoted in *The Times*, 30/3/83.

IS THERE TOO MUCH DIVERSITY?

Diversity exists within the system of public examinations at many levels. There is still a dual provision of examinations at 16+, although at 18+ GCE A level is almost unrivalled in schools. Within each national system – CSE, CEE and GCE O and A level – there are a number of providers offering different products. Within any subject there is a range of syllabuses covering different material and giving rise to different approaches to learning and assessment. Among the entrants for a particular subject there is often a great variety of experience, some candidates having meticulously followed the syllabus, others having ranged far beyond it. Individuals react differently to diversity in each of these areas and the challenge is to provide responsiveness without confusion.

Plans for a dramatic reduction in the number of examination boards at 16+ were formally abandoned following the 1979 general election. However, the collaborative efforts of those who have worked towards the introduction of the single system at 16+ may yet provide a more adequate answer to the question of diversity. This research has, though, indicated that the task of informing users needs to be added to the technical and administrative agenda. Much of the evidence in this report which underlined the need for a single 16+ qualification was offered in the form of an attack upon CSE. Little pressure was found outside the schools for a single system, but those working in industry and further and higher education attacked the content and conduct of CSE and were critical of the ability of those who had gained its qualification.

A number of factors indicated that the views which were expressed should be interpreted with caution. Few of those who responded in this way, particularly from higher education, appeared to acknowledge the claims for some form of recognition by the majority of secondary school students who would not be seeking higher education. Examinations, even at 16+, were rarely perceived by admissions staff in this wider context; many of those who were most critical of CSE actually made little or no use of the qualification in their process of selection. When encountered, CSE was often interpreted as a diluted GCE and few critical respondents offered anything other than a superficial knowledge of the qualities and skills of candidates holding a CSE certificate. Where practical experience was available, for example within school sixth forms, the methods employed in the preparation of candidates and the content of syllabuses which were more usually criticized and traditional perceptions of what comprises a subject became more important.

Those outside schools and sixth-form colleges provided numerous examples of misconceptions about the CSE examination, its target population, its syllabuses, its methods of examining and its certification. Such basic misinformation on the part of those professionally involved in examinations often also encompassed GCE. Many admissions tutors and selectors for employment appeared convinced, for example, that GCE O level was an appropriate test for all those in secondary schools.

At 18 + the status and functioning of GCE A level appeared almost unquestioned. A level dominated the selection of candidates for higher education and the variety of alternative systems was largely perceived as irrelevant. No case was made for a reduction in the range of alternative qualifications, perhaps because of their vocational implications; apparently, however, they were little used as entry qualifications and, from some questionnaire responses, it appeared that even mature students following non-traditional paths and offering alternative certification were treated with suspicion.

There were strong indications, particularly from the university sector in respect of A-level examinations, that the current diversity of boards, syllabuses and modes of examining is unwelcome. While a few recorded that they adjusted offers of places to take account of such factors, others wished that they were sufficiently well informed to do so. The folklore concerning 'hard' and 'easy' boards appear to have been subjected to little scrutiny although relevant evidence might, in many cases, have been extracted from students' entry and exit records.

While critical comment was directed at Mode III examinations by all types of user the approach was often inaccurately associated only with CSE. The weight of criticism gave a false impression of the frequency with which this mode of examining is adopted and by implication (spelled out clearly in a few cases), called into question the integrity and impartiality of teachers. The part played by examination boards in Mode III examinations appeared to be largely unrecognized and no critic drew the obvious parallels with the course content and the system of awards in higher education.

The diversity of subjects examined was identified as a problem mainly by employers although there were a few pleas for a rationalization of subject titles from those in further and higher education. Users from both sectors appeared to agree about the value of English language and arithmetic while making little use of examinations and syllabuses tailored to particular purposes, particularly in the scientific and technological areas.

Many admissions tutors recorded their interest in school differences. While in some cases an adjustment of offers was made in respect of known schools, known teachers and those having long-standing links with the institution, in other cases a form of positive discrimination based upon the headteacher's UCCA report of environmental, school or departmental problems was claimed.

A prevailing view on the place of diversity cannot be gained from such a range of practices and opinions. Certainly little was discovered to comfort those concerned to introduce a single system of examining at 16+. Examination boards will need to work hard to ensure users are accurately informed whether the dual system is retained or replaced, though it is difficult to suggest how this might be accomplished when users have taken so little account of the information already provided. There was similarly little evidence that information provided by the Standing Conference on University Entrance had penetrated the system. The attitudes of many users towards CSE and towards the lower grades of GCE gave some indication of the problem which would have to be overcome by any common grading system at 16+.

DO EXAMINATIONS DAMAGE THE SECONDARY SCHOOL CURRICULUM?

Almost from the inception of public examinations, fears have been expressed about the effect they might have upon the work of schools. Accounts of the damage they cause – currently expressed in terms of 'backwash' – are legion. Despite the experience at 16+ and 18+ testing and the evidence emerging on the effects of competency testing in the USA, such fears were echoed within the Project by a mere handful of respondents.

Examination boards make efforts to ensure that their syllabuses meet the requirements of schools and their students. Schools can select an appropriate syllabus or create one where all available syllabuses are unsuitable. An examination in a single subject can have only a modest constraining effect in a flexible and diverse system, though the impact of generating an educational programme by permutation from a range of single-subject examinations is clearly considerable. For many 16+ students education means examinations.

Also significant are the rather instrumental views of education often voiced by those outside the schools and the sometimes more sophisticated educational priorities of many working within the system. Society tends to downgrade that which is not examined or examinable and these effects can be reinforced by teachers. Most teachers, like most other professional groups, accept the importance attached to examinations; indeed, it is through examination that they have reached their present positions.

Alternative methods of fostering and validating ability or achievement are, in consequence, deemed suspect. Curriculum material which is not examined suffers a thousand minor cuts and teachers of non-examination groups traditionally have an uphill struggle to acquire resources and status.

Examinations remain an integral aspect of school accountability since they are accepted by parents and the community as respectable evidence of standards maintained. There is thus little incentive for teachers to extend their work beyond the often crowded examination syllabus or to take a greater responsibility for assessment. Where examinations are used as an excuse for not developing a more wide-ranging and responsive curriculum, where the unexamined is undervalued, and where an out-dated hierarchy of examination subjects is maintained, parents, employers and others who help to provide schools with their context, must accept part of the responsibility.

WHO SHOULD CONTROL EXAMINATIONS?

Examinations are presently controlled by the boards which, but for government intervention, would have been further reduced in number and changed in structure by amalgamation in connection with 16 + reform.*
As presently organized, the boards operate through collaboration between interest groups. Those included – representatives of higher education, further education, schools, industry, local and central government together with boards' professional staff – may form an unequal partnership but all views can be expressed. Some boards have, for example, recorded frustration over their failure to interest and actively to involve employers. Critics have pointed to the 'effective control' exerted by the universities.

It is clear that the role of teachers and schools in examining is not a dominant one despite the repeated emphasis on their importance in the reforms of recent years. In general, the views of users and the public towards teacher involvement in examining have been hostile. Mode III examining, as has been once again made clear in this report, has been construed as a dubious practice. Such views are often based on inadequate understanding of process and practice and an inaccurate perception of the number of candidates certificated through Mode III procedures.

Despite such problems it is clear that no single interest group should be

*Some fusion between boards has taken place, e.g. of The West Yorkshire and Lindsey Regional Examining Board and Yorkshire Regional Examinations Board to form the Yorkshire and Humberside Regional Examinations Board.

allowed to dominate examinations; the balance of interests requires continual review. The pervasive effect of undervaluing the contribution made by teachers was all too apparent from the research. Its effect can only be to constrain both the value of examinations and the effectiveness of teaching.

DO EXAMINATIONS PROVIDE AN ADEQUATE DESCRIPTION OF ACHIEVEMENT?

Aspects of this umbrella issue include what examinations measure, which populations they are designed to test, how results are recorded and how local and regional differences affect outcomes.

Examinations, by their nature, provide a limited description of performance. While the range of knowledge and skills which they test has been vastly extended in recent years and while the professional expertise available to the examination boards can (undoubtedly) be further extended, there are inevitable limits. The boundaries of what is possible are also reduced if examining is confined, in deference to user reserve, to familiar patterns. For example, evidence from this study would suggest that traditional external examinations miss opportunities to gain from wider and more pertinent assessments. The results of examinations are also currently presented as a single grade which subsumes wide variations of performance on different elements such as fields of knowledge and practical ability, though Harrison (1983) has suggested that more detailed breakdowns of different aspects of subject performance, while theoretically possible, are not within easy practical reach.

Examinations thus present a gross picture of a limited range of performance. This need not, of course, invalidate their results. There is a seemingly irresistible correlation between examination performances which to some extent overides subject differences. The question which schools could profitably address concerns the truth of the claim that it is really impossible to distinguish between that mass of unique individuals which constantly appears 'in the middle'. More doubts also arise in the area of the relationship between examination performance and subsequent progress.

The capacity of examinations to predict accurately subsequent achievement, whether this be in further examinations or in a work setting, is central to much of their use. Statistical correlations in these respects are, however, usually fairly weak. The 11+, for example, was eliminated as much for its predictive inefficiency as for social reasons. This test presents an interesting case history, since no better predictor of performance was found to replace it, and the same appears to be true of public examinations. Weak though their predictive capacity is, nothing has yet been used which provides more accurate prognostications. In the light of users' lack of trust in teachers, a replication of the Swedish meaned school marks approach (mentioned in Chapter I) appears impossible here.

Although at its introduction each examination had a target population, for whose needs the examination was tailored, the distinctions have become markedly blurred. The GCE O-level examination was designed for those in grammar schools (not a precisely defined population since it included widely variable proportions of the population from authority to authority). Those attending secondary modern schools were soon sitting and passing the examination and comprehensivization has probably extended the range of those attempting GCE. The population for which CSE was created was quickly supplemented with the raising of the school-leaving age. GCE A level has been colonized in much the same way by 'new sixth formers' undergoing conversion to more traditional routes and CEE has also been used to extend the experiences of conventional A-level candidates in a reverse migration. Lack of employment opportunity can only add further to the pressure on A level.

While such population drift might be seen as an admirable example of educational initiative it does pose problems in terms of the description of achievement which specific examinations can offer. In order to gain a stable standard over time, grading needs to be consistent and related to the performance of the original target population. Population drift makes this difficult since the basis for comparison is lost. Perhaps any reform dealing with something as volatile as achievement should be wary of the concept of a target population. Whatever is attempted it is clear that there can never be any acceptable method of identifying discrete ability groups for particular occupational or academic roles.

The research confirmed that study opportunities and subsequent examination performance varied substantially between schools. At least two views of the importance of school differences are current in higher education where such comparisons are most readily observable. One leads to selection on the principle that those who have done well will continue to achieve; the other notes that difficult school circumstances will depress examination performances but may have no long-term effect upon subsequent achievement. The second view suggests that examination results may provide a less than adequate description of achievement; certainly it acknowledges the reality that subsequent performance is at least as dependent upon future conditions as upon past experience.

An important factor influencing the usefulness of any examination certificate is its 'transfer value'. The possibility of introducing a formal mechanism to facilitate educational credit transfer has been explored at the level of higher education (DES, 1979b). It was also one of the many options considered by Locke and Bloomfield (1982) in their review of 16–19 provision. In its exploration of the acceptability of alternative qualifications at entry to higher education the current study has shown how individual actions can undermine formal procedures – in this case the attempts made by SCUE to establish equivalence and to permit a 'change of track' by individual students.

Although the evolution of the present system of public examinations partly reflects adverse judgements on the inappropriateness of grouped certification as a means of recording achievement, the approach is still widely used in the FE sector. Indeed, the CPVE is likely to embody group certification, and the issue is not therefore one which can be ignored.

Given that the minimal analysis which this study has shown tends to precede the use of examination results, it is in fact probable that many users would welcome grouped certification. It would provide a ready device of dividing applicants, although this would, of course, not necessarily focus on specific skills, knowledge or interests. While not ensuring that the 'right' candidates come forward it could rapidly reduce the numbers qualifying. While within schools grouped certification might be identified by some as an appropriate mechanism for more strongly endorsing a core curriculum, past experience suggests that its effect would be to further limit the educational experience of the majority.

For those at the transition points in education grouped certification could bring about a dramatic reduction in the chances of gaining validation of achievement. Many would gain no qualification and all would lose evidence of their individual strengths. Nor, as has recently been demonstrated yet again (DES, 1983), are records of achievement or pupil profiles yet able to fill the gap that would arise.

HOW ARE EXAMINATION RESULTS USED?

The study indicated that the uses made of examination results by industry and within education were not as distinctive as might have been expected. Some subjects inevitably had an almost vocational value in educational settings that they lacked in industry; otherwise, examinations were viewed and used in a remarkably similar way. In so far as examinations were identified as measures of general ability, they were seen as weakly predictive of future performance. Because such correlations were seen as of more direct significance within education they were accorded more importance. Even then, various permutations of grades and subjects were often regarded as acceptable.

Examinations were principally used to control numbers. They were used almost universally as a mechanism to screen out excess applicants, with the cut-off level being a function, among other factors, of the ratio of applicants to places. The association of entry level with course status was also not without influence. Because of the consistent way in which a proportion of candidates is allocated a particular grade, A level seems well-suited to use as a screen. An increase in the number of applicants or a decrease in the number of places can readily be handled. The resultant homogeneity in the qualifications of recruits, however, ensures that any relationship between examination grade and subsequent performance is masked.

Having been used to screen out excess numbers, examination results were then usually used to rank candidates to facilitate selection. The inevitable consequence of such practices was the grade inflation which was so clearly documented. Examples of such increases in the demands made upon applicants could be found among all types of user. Such procedures, while solving an administrative problem, put candidates under pressure by no means guaranteed to lead to improvement in examination performance.

Users often appeared to arrive at their selection criteria in response to the number of applicants confronting them rather than from attempts to match specific course or occupational demands with evidence of applicants' talents. In higher education particularly, potentially useful information – such as variations in performance in specific subject areas – was often lost by conflation. The 'points' systems employed do not have any obvious educational merit.

Only in crisis areas such as medicine, where numbers were influenced by central government, was the dilemma of too few places and too many applicants quite as stark as that facing much of industry. Specialist subjects apart, English and mathematics or, more accurately English language and arithmetic, appeared to reflect core requirements for both industry and education. There were few signs of any general wish on the part of users to see a wider education core including, for example, elements of science/ technology, humanities and craft.

Within educational settings a number of practices appeared to run counter to stated objectives and to the opinions expressed to the Project. Pass/fail grading was expressly rejected by the vast majority of respondents. However, in terms of their offers, many admissions tutors generated idiosyncratic pass/fail borderlines and thereby introduced a random factor into admissions.

The pressure for specialization within the sixth-form curriculum comes directly from the universities. Attempts to widen the curriculum have failed because a specialist base is claimed necessary for higher education. Yet in many institutions subject performance variation was hidden by the adding together of A-level grades and the use of this 'score' to determine entry. Such a practice severely undermines the case for specialist qualification. Where grade conflation is used, calls for more accurate measures of specialist attainment or more precise predications of performance would appear unwarranted.

A range of other selection criteria appeared to be applied by both industrial and educational users in a confident if rather haphazard way. While rejecting teacher assessments carefully built up over time (and often proffered with caution as to their subjectivity), many users claimed that they could elicit details of personality and behaviour in a brief interview. In educational settings there was little evidence of preparation for or coordination of this type of activity and while large companies may well train their selectors, it is doubtful if such training is undertaken by those working for smaller firms or educational institutions.

The criteria applied in such circumstances seemed sometimes to reflect preconceptions rather than analysis of the demands of the course or occupation. Indeed, indications of what these demands might be could usually only be divined in very generalized terms. Effective selection surely demands a careful and continuing analysis.

References and testimonials, especially those emanating from schools, were often treated with reserve and sometimes with outright suspicion. Such reactions are not guaranteed to encourage schools to provide more extensive and detailed documentation on pupils.

WHAT ALTERNATIVE FORMS OF ASSESSMENT AND REPORTING WOULD USERS WELCOME?

While there was almost total support for the retention of the present complex system of public examinations and no clear identification of performances about which more information was required, there was also considerable enthusiasm for a school-based profile or record of achievement to complement examination results.

In the light of present selection practices it is difficult to identify where such a contribution would most easily fit, although it might provide a satisfactory framework for interview. Whether a more formal structure would add weight to school-based documentation is uncertain but it is doubtful if anything which adds greatly to the complexity of selection would readily achieve acceptance within the present system. Certainly, before more detailed information about applicants could be fully exploited users would need to re-evaluate their requirements and procedures.

Making better use of examinations

The preceding review of issues has underlined, once again, that a concerted effort on the part of practitioners and policy makers is needed to achieve change. Users of examination results, although likely to benefit from this activity, also need to reconsider their own processes. There were some indications that structural change was necessary but much more obvious was the need to change attitudes. Many users' comments implied doubts concerning the value of examination results which, if widespread, would make examinations work a poor investment for students, for schools, and for LEAs. Nothing convincing has so far been suggested which could fill the gaps examinations would leave: gaps in the curriculum structure, in motivation for many students, in purpose for many schools – maintained and independent – gaps, too, in accountability and in the process of accreditation. In a period of such rapid social and educational change, where long-term priorities are difficult to identify, where so little consensus for change exists and where incremental improvements are already in hand, global change appears inappropriate. What is offered, therefore, is a series of suggestions – an agenda to help bring the system of public examinations more in line with current needs.

Suggestions for teachers and educational institutions

1 Review examinations policy and identify institutional factors which influence opportunity and limit examination success. These might include:

a the criteria used to set, stream or band students;
b the extent to which grouping practices determine opportunity;
c the extent to which the (core) curriculum keeps options open for all students;
d the action taken to avoid racial, sexual, socioeconomic or subject stereotyping when students choose or are routed to subjects and examinations;
e the regularity with which syllabuses are evaluated and updated;
f the policy concerning fees in respect of double or repeat entry.

2 Review the needs of students and establish ways of ensuring that they are well-informed about examinations and their use. For example, they should understand:

a the demands made by different examination courses in different subjects;
b the currency of different qualifications in different subjects;
c how to develop the skills needed to handle study, library work, discussion, presentation, decision, revision and examinations;
d how to make the most of the institution's learning resources;
e the way in which performance is assessed and reported throughout the institution and in public examinations;
f how to interpret assessments, reports and certificates;
g how to monitor their own performance;
h how to evaluate their own qualities and establish new goals.

3 Review the needs of teachers and devise ways of extending their expertise in:
a curriculum analysis, planning and development in order to give due weight to cross-curricular and within-subject balance between experience, skills, knowledge, understanding and attitudes;
b establishing criteria against which to assess student performance;
c operating a wide range of assessment techniques including testing, examining, rating, scoring, standardizing, monitoring, negotiating and goal-setting;
d diagnosing students' strengths, weaknesses and interests and identifying appropriate measures for support;
e guiding pupils on subject choice, examination entry and the skills necessary to succeed;
f making and monitoring accurate predictions of examination performance;
g preparing records, reports and references which pay due regard to examinations among other sources of information.

4 Initiate discussions with staff, parents, students, governors, nearby schools, further and higher education institutions and local employers to extend understanding of:

a the qualities of pupils not tested by examinations;
b the value of a broad curriculum;
c the contribution of different curriculum areas;
d the contribution of different examination subjects;
e the standards associated with different examinations and different grades;
f the institution's policy on assessment, examinations and reporting;

g the ways in which the institution is able to extend, enrich and supplement information on student achievement.

Suggestions for local government administrators, advisers and inspectors

1 Discuss with teachers their in-service needs with respect to:

a curriculum analysis, planning and development;
b examinations policy, assessment, recording and reporting;
c grouping and selection procedures;
d student guidance and counselling.

2 Identify and provide sources of expertise to meet needs in appropriate ways. Help will be found among:

a teachers with extensive experience in curriculum or examinations work;
b LEA advisory staff and local HM Inspectorate;
c local establishments of further and higher education;
d professional and subject associations;
e examination boards;
f national research and development agencies.

3 Work to increase the understanding of users of examination results. Activities should be aimed at selectors in:

a sixth forms and sixth-form colleges;
b tertiary colleges and colleges of further education;
c colleges of higher education, polytechnics and universities;
d commerce, public service and industry.

Suggestions for central government

1 Encourage examining boards to:

a work collaboratively to coordinate and rationalize their provision and procedures;
b reform examinations at 16+, 17+ and 18+ to meet changing needs;
c rationalize the range of syllabuses and subject titles at all levels;
d make use of the full range of available assessment techniques;
e investigate grading procedures, particularly at A level.

2 Stimulate and support local authorities as they seek to:

a identify and meet in-service needs;
b locate and deploy sources of expertise;
c improve users' understanding.

3 Initiate and support continued research and development work in connection with:

a examinations at 16 + and 18 +;
b extending the range of assessment and reporting practices;
c the appropriate use of examinations and other sources of information for selection.

Suggestions for examining boards

1 Review the roles played by teachers at all levels, local authorities and employers in the workings of the board. Establish structures which provide a proper influence on:

a board policy, administration, finance and publications;
b examination arrangements including modes of examining, marking, moderating, awarding, certification and appeals;
c developments in syllabuses and assessment techniques;
d the maintenance of standards.

2 Contribute to the development of expertise in examination centres by:

a providing publications aimed at professionals;
b involving teachers increasingly in syllabus development and assessment;
c contributing to seminars and workshops for teachers.

3 Help to improve public understanding of examinations by:

a providing publications aimed at a wide audience;
b extending the involvement of the various interest groups in board operations;
c contributing to public discussion on examinations.

4 Improve existing examinations by:
a rationalizing examination titles and syllabuses;

b employing regularly reviewed general and subject criteria at all levels of examining;
c seeking greater consistency of approach to moderation, coursework, borderline review, disadvantaged candidates and appeals;
d making use of the full range of assessment techniques;
e monitoring the use made of examination results.

Suggestions for users of examination results

1 Review thoroughly the present examinations system. In particular, explore:

a the range and nature of available public examinations;
b the way examination boards function and the relationships between them; the way syllabuses and examinations are created;
c the meaning of subject titles and the nature of syllabuses;
d the range of assessment techniques, the virtues and shortcomings of each approach;
e the nature of the grading scales and their meanings.

2 Examine the range of alternative sources of information about applicants. In particular consider the origins and strengths of:

a school records, references and testimonials;
b candidates' self-evaluations and records of achievement;
c examination certificates;
d application forms – their structure, content and interpretation;
e test materials – their suitability, validity, reliability, conduct, marking criteria and interpretation;
f interviews, their purpose, conduct and validity;
g informal and 'off the record' information.

3 Establish training programmes to help selectors:

a identify the skills, knowledge, understanding and attitudes required by recruits;
b determine appropriate means for gathering relevant evidence;
c recognize evidence of appropriate qualities in applicants;
d develop evaluative skills; include those needed for interviewing;
e ensure careful monitoring of selection criteria against subsequent performance;

f encourage the provision of up-to-date information concerning selection procedures to applicants, schools and colleges.

It is clear that these suggestions do not offer an instant escape for those trapped within the maze of the public examination system. Nor do they present users with a ready solution to all their problems. If pursued, however, they do offer the promise of a greater rationality, where candidates may receive improved guidance and users are better able to fulfil their expectations.

Appendices

Appendix A Project information

Table 1 *Number of interviews and telephone interviews shown by sector*

Sector	Number of interviews
Schools and sixth-form colleges	21
Colleges of further education	22
Polytechnics	14
Universities	30
Other (including examining boards)	6
Total	93

Table 2 *Sample size and rate of response shown by sector*

Users	Sample size	Respondents	% response
Schools and sixth-form colleges	1082	784	72
Colleges of further education	226	209	92
Colleges of higher education	25	25	100
Polytechnics	27	26	96
Universities	60	45	75
Employers	1417	494	35

Table 3 *Schools with sixth forms and sixth-form colleges participating in the study*

Type of institution	Number	%
Comprehensive schools	516	66
Grammar schools	76	10
Secondary modern schools	18	2
Other (including bilateral)	15	2
Independent schools	133	17
Sixth-form colleges	26	3
Totals	784	100

Table 4 *Sample size and response rate shown by sector*

	Sample size	Respondents	% response
GCE A-level courses			
Schools and sixth-form colleges	1082	864	80
Colleges of further education	93	67	72
Colleges of higher education	7	6	86
Totals	1182	937	79
Other non-advanced courses			
Colleges of further education	362	267	74
Colleges of higher education	33	6	18
Polytechnics	5	5	100
Totals	400	278	70
Degree courses			
Colleges of higher and further education	30	17	57
Polytechnics	151	100	66
Universities	526	326	62
Totals	707	443	63
Other advanced courses			
Colleges of further education	16	8	50
Colleges of higher education	24	16	67
Polytechnics	61	43	70
Totals	101	67	66

Table 5 *Non-degree courses in colleges of further and higher education included in the study*

Non-advanced courses other than GCE

College-based courses

Foundation Art and Design
General Secretarial
Pre-nursing
Pre-professional Art

Externally Validated Courses

Association of Medical Secretaries, Practice Administrators and Receptionists:	Diploma in Medical Secretarial Studies
Business Education Council:	General Diploma in Business Studies
	General Diploma in Distribution
	National Diploma in Business Studies
	National Diploma in Financial Studies
	National Diploma in Public Administration
City and Guilds of London Institute:	Basic Engineering Craft Studies – Part I, Mechanical (Course 200)
	Basic Engineering Process Studies (Mechanical) (Course 200)
	Foundation Course in Community Care (Course 689)
	Foundation Course in Community Care and Home Economics (Course 689)
	General Catering Course (Course 705)
	Hairdressing – Certificate in Ladies Hairdressing (Course 760)
London Chamber of Commerce and Industry:	Private Secretary's Certificate
	Secretarial Studies Certificate
National Council for Home Economics Education:	Certificate in Home Management and Family Care
National Nursery Examination Board:	Certificate of the NNEB
Ordinary National Diploma:	Hotel and Catering Operations
	Sciences
	Technical
Technician Education Council:	Diploma in Building Studies
	Diploma in Building and Civil Engineering Studies
	Diploma in Civil Engineering Studies

Diploma in Hotel, Catering and
Institutional Operations
Diploma in Science
Diploma in Technology (Engineering)

Advanced Courses

College-based courses
Foundation Accountancy*

Externally validated courses
Business Education Council: Higher National Diploma in Business Studies
Higher National Diploma in Financial Studies
Higher National Diploma in Public Administration
Higher National Diploma: Applied Biology
Applied Physics
Building
Computer Studies
Electrical and Electronic Engineering
Food Technology
Hotel and Catering Administration
Mathematics, Statistics and Computing
Mechanical Engineering
Metallurgy
Production Engineering
Technician Education Council: Higher Diploma in Building Studies
Higher Diploma in Civil Engineering Studies
Higher Diploma in Electronics
Higher Diploma in Mechanical and Production Engineering
Higher Diploma in Metallurgical Studies
Higher Diploma in Physical Sciences (Chemistry)
Higher Diploma in Physical Sciences (Physics)
Council for National Academic Awards† Diploma in Higher Education

---

* A few of these courses are also externally validated.
† Validated either by CNNA or one of the universities.

Table 6 *Titles of degree courses included in the study**

Accountancy
Accountancy Studies
Accounting and Finance
Accounting and Financial
    Management
Accounting and Financial Studies
Accounting and Law
Anthropology and Psychology
Anthropology and Sociology
Applied Biological Sciences
Applied Biology
Applied Economics
Applied Human Biology
Applied Physics
Architectural Design
Architecture
Architecture and
    Environmental Design
Art
Art History Studies
B.Ed.
Biological Sciences
Biological Studies
Biology
Biophysical Science
Building
Building Construction and
    Management
Building Technology and
    Management
Business Administration
Business Studies
Chemical and Administrative
    Science
Chemical Engineering
Chemistry
Chemistry and Management
    Studies
Civil and Architectural
    Engineering
Civil Engineering
Classical Studies and
    Sociology
Computation
Computational Science
Computer Science
Computer Studies
Computing Science
Computing Studies
Creative Design
Dentistry
Economics
Economics and Mathematics
Economics and Public Policy
Education
Educational Studies
Educational Studies and Drama
Electrical and Electronic Engineering
Electrical Engineering
Electrical Engineering including
    Electronics
Electrical Engineering Science
Engineering
Engineering Electronics
Engineering Production and Economics
Engineering Science and Management
Engineering with German
English
English and History
English Language and Literature
English Literature
English Studies
Environmental Sciences
European History and Philosophy
European Languages and Institutions
Finance and Accounting
Fine Art
French
French and Arabic
French Language and Literature
French Language with Sociology
French Studies

General Architectural Studies
Geography and Management
 Studies
Geological Sciences
Geology
German and Danish
German and Drama
German and Russian
German with Italian
Historical Studies
History
History of Art
History of Art and
 Architecture
Industrial Biology
Industrial Technology and
 Management
Italian and European Literature
Landscape Architecture
Language and Education
Language and Linguistics
Law
Legal Studies
Linguistics
Linguistics and Phonetics
Management Science
Managerial and Administrative
 Studies
Mathematical Science
Mathematical Studies with
 Education
Mathematics
Mathematics and Language
Mathematics and Management Science
Mathematics and Operational Research
Mathematics and Psychology
Mathematics and Statistics
Mathematics, Statistics and
 Computing
Medicine
Medieval and Modern History
Medieval English and History
Metallurgical Engineering and
 Management
Metallurgy and Management
Metallurgy and Mechanical
 Engineering
Modern Language Studies
Modern Languages
Philosophy and Art
Physical Education
Physical Education and Sports Science
Physical Electronics
Physics
Property Valuation and Management
Psychology and Sociology
Pure Mathematics
Pure Mathematics and Language
 Studies
Russian and Sociology
Social History and Sociology
Social Sciences
Social Studies
Sociology
Sociology with Professional
 Management
Systems and Information Management
Textile Design and Management
Textiles and Design
Veterinary Science
Visual Arts.

---

* Degree titles may not always clearly indicate the nature of the course content.

Appendix B Admissions to Oxford and Cambridge

Traditionally, students at Oxford and Cambridge are members of a college and only incidentally students of the university. More directly, because admissions are conducted by colleges rather than by subject departments or faculties, these two universities present a very different pattern of selection to that already described in the rest of higher education. Many would also claim that Oxford and Cambridge enrol the academically most able undergraduates and therefore form the most highly selective pinnacles of a very selective system. While most would agree that this intention underlies the admissions procedures at Oxford and Cambridge not all (including admissions tutors at these two universities) are so certain that the process of selection achieves this objective.

Alone among the institutions providing higher education, Oxford and Cambridge have continued to use an entrance examination as the major selection device. This has, in recent years, not offered the only route to an Oxford or Cambridge place but it has remained the most important. The entrance examination is held in the autumn of the year preceding admission and the Oxford papers are marked and selection completed by the end of that term, Cambridge admissions being brought to a conclusion about a month later.

Candidates in former years were normally students who had completed a two-year sixth-form course and who had remained a further term within their schools in order to take the examination. This timing allowed preparatory work (coaching) to take place. More recently 'fourth-term students' still working towards the GCE A-level examination have formed a proportion of those taking the examination and 'seventh-term' candidates have steadily declined in numbers. Although most parents and many schools speak of 'preparing for the Oxbridge Examination' there are two quite separate sets of papers. What was quickly confirmed by discussions with a number of admissions tutors was that the examination was but one aspect of the variety of approaches to selection and that there were almost as many procedures in use as there were colleges.

The collegiate system, with all that it implies for teaching methods and for the socialization of students, is central to this approach to higher education. It necessarily has a marked effect upon selection. The very complexity of entrance procedures confirms the confidence of those endowed with 'received wisdom', be they teachers guiding the choice of applicants or applicants themselves.

Tutors pointed out that 'the system' was essentially developed when candidates came from the relatively small number of independent and grammar schools where the majority of the teaching staff were themselves Oxford and Cambridge graduates. Although secondary education has changed in fundamental ways, the 'Oxbridge network' remains a vital link for many colleges.

College-based recruitment also directly affects the range of subject options open to applicants, particularly where colleges are small. The team was provided with a number of illustrations of the ways in which this worked. A sought-after course in a popular college required far higher standards of admission from its candidates than the same course approached through a less popular college: 'at the end of the day marginal people may be unlucky but good candidates always get into one or other college'. There were quite marked differences between Oxford and Cambridge in this respect and an 'unlucky' choice of Cambridge college appeared far more likely to result in failure to obtain a place. The position could be exacerbated where the college was small or when a college did not have a teaching fellow in the particular subject area. The inclination, particularly at present when numbers are being actively cut back, was to 'feed the fellows', ensuring that college tutors received an adequate number of students in their subject speciality, often at the expense of minority subjects. The Oriental Studies and Fine Arts Courses at Oxford were said to be at risk because of this sort of action. Representatives of minority subjects were, in consequence, becoming more directly involved in selection. At Cambridge there was also evidence of 'faculty intrusion' in selection, particularly on the part of the larger subject disciplines, although individually some admissions tutors resented and resisted these moves. The balance between the choice of the college and the wishes of the subject groups was variously interpreted:

[It is] complicated for the faculties who have no control over intake.

[There are] some difficulties in that the colleges work individually.

[It is] true that one's faculty impinges on feelings about admissions.

When there is talk of faculty admissions, ... hackles rise.

The university is exercising more and more say on admissions.

Autonomy is quite real and there is nothing the university could do if, for example, we decided not to take any classicists.

College autonomy is a bit of an illusion.

Over the years Oxford and Cambridge have been subjected to a number of political and educational criticisms and have consequently received considerable attention from the media. Much of the criticism has been directed at the selection process. In the two years of the Project's life, apart from the usual 'league tables' devoted to recording the recruitment from state and independent schools, there appeared comparisons of: the quality of degree obtained by students originating

APPENDIX B 143

from the maintained and independent sectors; reports on the differential use of conditional and matriculation offers by various colleges; attacks upon the use of an entrance examination and upon the universities' unwillingness to change. The Labour Party also issued a critique of the selection process and implied that unless reforms were voluntarily undertaken they would be introduced by a future Labour government.

Such media coverage necessarily gave rise to a range of reactions within the institutions themselves. Some admissions tutors saw such 'reporting' as a causal factor contributing to inequality by arousing the very prejudice which inhibits applications from the maintained sector. An Oxford undergraduate investigation of the selection procedures largely agreed with this proposition, pointing to the impossibility of selecting maintained school students when they did not apply. Others have, perhaps more pragmatically, agreed that to attempt to make selection equitable is not sufficient – it must also be accepted as such by observers. A number of schools and colleges contributing to this study amply demonstrated the issue: 'We do not encourage people to apply for Oxbridge. Very rarely do we get anyone of that calibre anyway.' (sixth-form college). The alternative to voluntary reform, an imposed quota of undergraduates from maintained schools, was seen as a very undesirable, although a conceivable future option.

What was clear was that considerable changes had taken place in admissions to both Oxford and Cambridge in recent years. A brief review of one of these major changes, the opening of the Oxford colleges to women illustrates the inherent inertia and radicalism which coexist within such a decentralized organization. The example underlines the essentially 'federal' nature of the collegiate university and the combination of idealism and self-interest which leads to the making and breaking of alliances within that federation.

In the early 1960s there was no feeling that anything dramatic should happen. It was considered sufficient to increase the number of women at Oxford by subsidising women's colleges. Within two or three years there was a sudden move away from this position. Two colleges (New College and Balliol) suggested opening their selection to women but they were opposed by others. As a result five colleges (Jesus, Brasenose, St Catherines, Hertford and Wadham) collaborated in the design of a five-year experiment to introduce and gradually increase the number of women undergraduates. Once it became clear that the experiment was working, other colleges expressed a wish to adopt the same policy. Within a common meeting it was agreed that applications from women should be introduced by batches of five to eight colleges at a time. One or two colleges then decided, in closed meetings, not to go mixed. The reaction to this was a decision, by about twenty colleges, probably taken collectively, to go mixed overnight. Undoubtedly pressure from those colleges at the end of the queue contributed towards the rapidity of the change. By 1983 one college remained all-male and there were three colleges recruiting only women, although a number of the formerly male colleges were still seen by others as 'reluctantly mixed'. What often emerged in discussion was that, in some cases at least, the policy change had had little to do with ideas of equity and justice and much more to do with the maintenance of a sufficient number of high-calibre candidates.

Although the movement towards mixed colleges at Cambridge was more or less contemporaneous with the change at Oxford there was far less coordination and a considerable element of intercollege rivalry for good candidates. The outcome of these changes was not easy to evaluate. Although the proportion of women undergraduates in Cambridge had increased to more than 30 per cent, it was pointed out by tutors that mixing had led to a decline in the number of women attempting more adventurous courses and a reassertion of the stereotype – male engineers and female artists. The number of applicants to those women's colleges remaining fell and this exacerbated the very lumpy distribution of applicants to courses which already existed. Discussions with tutors confirmed continued advantages in attending a women's college identified in terms of the wider role models that were offered, the privacy, the reduction of social competition and 'for those that want it, a strong feminist tradition'.

The differential patterns of reform in Oxford and Cambridge were confirmed by tutors, particularly where these had graduated from one university and were working in the other. Oxford was typified by much greater cooperation between colleges in matters such as agreeing the selection policy and transferring applicants where potential personality clashes might inhibit the full demonstration of academic capacity. A number of Oxford tutors expressed the view that the particular college to which an applicant was eventually attached was relatively unimportant. Intercollege competition was much more in evidence in Cambridge and in a few cases it became clear that a potential clash of personality at interview was sufficient reason for the outright rejection of an application rather than as a case for intercollege transfer. Professional contacts between admissions tutors at Cambridge, as judged by their knowledge of each others' procedures, were not frequent. The closer ties between Oxford colleges did, however, also lead to an inhibition of reform on some occasions. The publicly announced attempt by Keble College to modify the use of offers in the current cycle of admissions was described as 'naughty' by other colleges, chiefly because it was only revealed when it was too late for any other college to adopt it. The way in which the scheme was proposed was viewed with horror, and Keble was asked to postpone the plan. The negotiations were described as 'touch and go' with the ultimate sanction of exclusion from the prospectus being threatened. The power of intercollegiate links ensured that non-conformity would have made 'life very difficult and ... quite shattered Keble'.

There were no ambiguities concerning the role of admissions tutors at Oxford or Cambridge; all saw the task as a vital one and the collegiate structure ensured that a tutor would routinely be faced with the results of any incorrect decision. Many college tutors in both Oxford and Cambridge described their efforts to establish contact with a wider range of schools in the maintained sector. The Oxford Admissions Office was also involved in considerable school contacts. One Cambridge tutor expressed the position as one where 'we are very concerned not to be a finishing school for the wealthy aristocracy ... but we do believe in intellectual elitism ...'.

The nature of the contacts included:

> writing directly to schools;
> writing to schools via local authority advisers;
> invitations to open days (teachers, headteachers and pupils);
> attending school and local authority careers conferences;
> contacting the schools of all previous candidates;
> headteacher weekends: e.g. 30 sixth-form college principals chosen at random;
> contacting all secondary schools in a region which had previously provided few candidates.

Although tutors were able to record some success, many of these efforts had received a minimal response and one tutor reported such hostility from a teachers' centre audience that a repetition of that attempt was unlikely.

Admissions tutors received information on candidates from their own application form and from the UCCA form. Because the latter was completed at a rather later date it was often looked at to see if prediction of grades had changed. The information on a candidate's family background was sometimes referred to on the UCCA form since it 'could not possibly be included on the university form'. The UCCA form was also used by some admissions tutors to identify candidates' choice of course in other universities.

Information about candidates from the independent sector was often passed directly to the tutor and although some headteachers obviously attempted to influence entry decisions this was seen as largely ineffective. Links with individual headteachers were valued by most tutors and their judgement of a candidate was seen as accurate. The other major source of information was the entrance examination. The 'flavour' of this can be most readily conveyed by a General Paper, three questions from which had to be attempted in three hours:

GENERAL PAPER

Answer three questions. Question 26 [not included here] is compulsory for candidates wishing to read Literae Humaniores or Modern Languages or a combined Honour School which includes Modern Languages; it is optional for all other candidates. Candidates wishing to read Law are advised to answer at least one of questions 21–25; these questions may also be answered by other candidates.

1. Examine the case for censorship in the arts.
2. 'Cease to use your hands and you have lopped off a huge chunk of your consciousness' (George Orwell). Discuss.
3. 'Industrial society, unlike the commercial, craft and agrarian societies which it replaces, does not need the past.' Do you agree?
4. What does it mean to assert 'sovereignty' over disputed territory?
5. 'To dissociate literary criticism from politics is itself to adopt a political position.' Discuss.

6. Has the study of history rather than that of the natural sciences posed the greater threat to religious beliefs?
7. 'We have the same obligations towards the generation of human beings that will be living in the thirty-first century as we have towards those in the twenty-first.' Discuss.
8. EITHER: Is there anything to be said for Carlyle's view of history as 'the biography of great men'?

   OR: 'Curiosity is never more agreeably or usefully employed than in examining the laws and customs of foreign nations' (Samuel Johnson). Discuss.
9. 'It is symptomatic of our time that we can value a work of art for its complexity, but not for its simplicity.' Discuss.
10. Explain and illustrate the difference in meaning between any six of the following pairs of words:
    i. infer; imply
    ii. flout; flaunt
    iii. simple; simplistic
    iv. sensual; sensuous
    v. militate; mitigate
    vi. licence; license
    vii. sympathy; empathy
    viii. efficient; efficacious
    ix. pity; mercy
    x. temporal; temporary
11. Does it matter whether life evolved on the earth or came to earth from outer space?
12. Consider the view that arguments for the existence of God convince only those who already believe in him.
13. 'Mathematicians are like Frenchman; whatever you say to them they translate into their own language and forthwith it is something entirely different' (Goethe). Discuss.
14. 'Qualitative thinking is of no value to a scientist.' Discuss.
15. 'To say "all men are equal" is just to make a meaningless noise.' Is it?
16. 'The televised sequence of Shakespeare's plays is the standard version for the 1980s.' Discuss.
17. EITHER: Should the historian believe in progress?

    OR: Is there anything to be said for Macaulay's view that, 'As civilization advances, poetry almost necessarily declines?'
18. 'It is easy to calculate the cost of higher education but impossible to estimate the value.' Discuss.
19. How would you present the evidence for atoms and molecules to an intelligent layman?
20. The fundamental defect of fathers is that they want their children to be a credit to them' (Bertrand Russell). Discuss.
21. What do you understand by 'positive discrimination?' Is it ever justified?
22. Is there any justification in present circumstances for requiring a divorced man to continue to support his former wife financially?
23. 'If one holds that it would be wrong, in all circumstances, actually to use strategic nuclear weapons, one must also hold that it is wrong to threaten to use them.' Discuss.
24. What are the purposes of the punishment of criminals? Do you think that any of these purposes are in fact achieved?

25. Should public transport be subsidized? If so, should this be from national or local taxation?

(The Colleges of Oxford Joint Scholarship and Entrance Examination, General Paper 1982. Reproduced by permission.)

Question 26 involved the reduction of a 720-word passage to one of less than 250 words and the production of comment on either its argument or its style. Questions on other papers ranged broadly across their subject and in many cases were framed to allow the maximum diversity of response.

The publicly stated case for a special entrance examination has frequently centred upon two aspects: that such an examination can be designed to provide the maximum of helpful information to assist in selection, and that it provides a unique opportunity for those selecting to see examples of the candidate's unaided work. There were distinct differences in the degree to which these rationales could be supported by evidence from the two universities.

The Oxford examination had been common to all colleges since 1963; in Cambridge one individual college examination – a multidisciplinary paper at New Hall – had survived. In both Oxford and Cambridge the range of alternative papers was currently being reduced although opinions among Cambridge tutors were divided about whether this was primarily to simplify the system for applicants or to reduce the effect of rising costs. (At Cambridge any shortfall in the funds raised by the fee was met by colleges in proportion to the number of candidates sitting the examination, at Oxford the fee covered the cost of the examination and its administration.) Many from both universities agreed with the view that:

On the whole the examination does the job well. Fewer papers will [simplify] marking but I am not sure whether it will make the setting of the papers any easier.

Panels of subject tutors produced the papers in both universities although, particularly at Cambridge, some doubts were raised about the suitability of some of the volunteers involved in the setting of papers, since they were often 'not senior people'. The view was expressed that some things that had happened, for example, in the science examination, were 'frankly appalling' since the designers 'had little experience of school-based exams ... the Cambridge Common Entrance is much more a pre-tripos examination'. Other Cambridge tutors took the view that because the examination was 'set by people who set the tripos it gives an idea of aptitude to cope with the course ...'.

Many Oxford and Cambridge admissions tutors acknowledged that the examination had improved considerably over the years although there was a vociferous minority who witheld their expertise from its creation and criticized the work of others. A number of those interviewed described the problems encountered in the preparation of the examination:

We worry constantly about the level of the papers ... they should look easier for pre-A-level candidates ... The paper should be 'do-able' but feedback from schools is limited ... What feedback we do get suggests that we are not too far off.

The hope was also expressed that those setting the papers would take account of the variety of examining boards and syllabuses.

Distinctions were frequently drawn between the relative ease of examining in 'science and mathematics' and the difficulty encountered in producing appropriate questions in the 'humanities and literary subjects' where so much 'depends on background reading'. Such problems were seen as particularly acute in the case of fourth-term candidates when the inevitably partial and differential coverage of the A-level texts was exacerbated by the relative immaturity of the candidates:

> The questions remain the same, only the answers are different. It is very difficult to be sure that this pre-A-level, less developed candidate, is better than the more sophisticated post-A-level candidate.

> I prefer our own examination ... [where] I can look for potential and imagination ... Even if an applicant has given a 'wrong' answer he might still be an interesting candidate whom I would want to interview.

Perhaps inevitably, this approach was identified as bringing about a greater recruitment of seventh-term candidates in English where 'breadth of reading', 'maturity' and 'sophistication' were described as affecting the measurement of 'creativity and flair'. The reverse pattern of recruitment, with most successful candidates being in their fourth term, was identified in science and mathematics. Both universities made use of 'school teacher' or university department moderators to widen their views of the process. There were wide differences between the way completed scripts were treated in the two universities.

In Cambridge 'teams' of markers completed the task. Although markers were nominated by colleges and the process was identified by some as an 'essential loss of freedom' in the cause of 'objectivity', others were more critical, pointing out that marking was 'very much a chore' and 'the price paid for central marking and a common standard has been to make it harder to look at scripts'. It was clear that, although there was no official barrier preventing access to completed scripts, they were rarely looked at. Where they were scrutinized it was more likely to be by arts tutors than mathematicians or science tutors although the general paper was occasionally searched by such directors of studies for evidence of a candidate's 'personal' or 'individual' qualities. The marking team provided a grade for each paper and notes were added 'on the arts side'. These varied in extent from such cryptic comments as 'short work' to a full half page of notes, detailing particular features of the candidate's performance. Marking was completed without marking guides:

> blind – in vacuo ... marking every script to the same standard, making no allowance for anything ... not even illness ... schools are given numbers not names ... background circumstances ... we cannot make allowances for any of these things.

Only when it came to 'deciding on ordinary places' did background factors receive 'very serious attention' at Cambridge.

The marking of scripts at Oxford remained in the hands of the subject tutors and this was identified as a particular strength of their approach.

Scripts are marked by tutors of the college of first preference except for mathematics, where they are marked by the faculty, and some minority subjects where they are marked at departmental level ... [the marking] is a perceptive assessment of the nitty gritty stuff ... an integral part of the selection process ... performance is 'weighted' for no-coaching, poor teaching, background, etc. You sum up and say that given the circumstances this candidate has done very well ... you have to weigh up apparent brilliance of mind with lack of knowledge.

Not everyone agreed that it was possible to make allowances for the full range of factors such as social and educational background and age.

All you can really do if a fourth and a seventh termer both write a beta plus script is to give the edge to the fourth termer. But if the seventh termer has a better mark ... that's that. We feel ourselves we are marking on potential but I don't see how we can really do it.

Whereas in Cambridge the cycle of examinations was most usually followed by a largely private transaction, what followed the Oxford examinations was more frequently described in terms appropriate to the auction room. The successful Cambridge examinee was offered a place in the selected college. In Oxford the very able candidates were more widely distributed allowing even the small colleges within a group to receive some.

Both universities then made use of a pool system where possibly suitable candidates who had thus far failed to obtain a place were considered by all other colleges. A further 'pool' operated for those remaining in 'the system' but still unplaced after the publication of the A-level results. Cambridge colleges made considerable use of the pool and even the 'summer pool' was used by some to make up a shortfall of conditional-offer students. In Oxford the pool appeared to act as a safety net and the view was expressed that 'personal contacts were more effective'. Although there was a 'common pool', theoretically shared by both Oxford and Cambridge, the take-up of candidates from this source was so rare as to render the procedure insignificant.

Apart from the perennial problem of ensuring the recruitment of the very ablest candidates, dissatisfaction with the ability of the entrance examination to attract and select able candidates from the maintained sector had caused a number of colleges in both univerisites to use alternative approaches. The proportion of applicants selected by other methods varied widely between colleges. However, wherever the system of 'offers' was used it essentially depended upon predictions of GCE A-level results. The majority of colleges in both Oxford and Cambridge used the system of conditional offers as already described for other institutions, but some made use of 'matriculation offers'. There appeared to be an almost universal acceptance of the use of the conditional offer, even where these were seen as a less accurate way of identifying suitable students. While it was postulated that all applicants obtained such good grades that these did not discriminate, conditional offers were not seen as unethical.

The reaction to matriculation offers was often more extreme. Supporters of the system saw the matriculation offer as encouraging able applicants who might otherwise be deterred by a lack of suitable sixth-form teaching or by unrealistic fears of the system. It was also identified as giving A-level candidates the confidence to relax and thus ensure a high standard of performance at 18+. Critics spoke of matriculation offers as a 'confidence trick', designed to capture the most able but selecting them on fairly doubtful information. It was a 'trick' because almost all of those who received matriculation offers were expected to achieve very good A-level results. A few critics offered the opinion that it must be a bad thing to so 'take the pressure off' sixth formers and that it would inevitably lead to a decline in A-level performance. Although there was anecdotal evidence available to confirm the first proposition none was offered in support of the second. Some colleges, making a small number of matriculation offers, limited them to candidates who would not achieve the normal entry conditions because of a disadvantaged background but who would 'be able to cope with the course'. This was acknowledged as 'a PR exercise'.

Although in each university the use of conditional offers was an attempt to increase the range of applicants and ensure that the most able would be recruited from whatever source, there were quite clear differences in the offers made by the two universities. Admissions tutors at Cambridge who were involved in this process commonly expressed the view that: 'although A level does not test exactly what we are looking for ... if [the candidates] do not get good A's they will not succeed'. A rather more extreme view was that A level must be 'intrinsically better than the amateur [entrance] examination'. The common wisdom, however, suggested that 'if a college makes a lot of conditional offers it has got to pitch high', effectively establishing a new barrier. Cambridge conditional offers were therefore often limited to A grades and frequent use was made of high grades achieved on Special Papers to ensure the maximum discrimination. Such situations could result in offers demanding A1, A1, A or A1, A1, B, and anecdotal evidence was offered for an increasing number of applicants offering four A levels. Some admissions tutors were rather suspicious of such candidates, doubting that such pressures were likely to be beneficial in the long term.

Realistically, a number of tutors pointed out that maintained schools unable to offer support to candidates attempting the entrance examination would be unlikely to have the necessary resources to enter candidates for S levels. One tutor recorded his doubts over taking 'a marginal and suspect candidate with A2, A2, B when conditional offers were adjusted in August'. Where fewer conditional offers were made they did not usually include S levels nor did they set such high conditions. One tutor reported that he had looked unsuccessfully for statistical correlation between S level and tripos results (mathematics).

Essentially, in Cambridge, whether the numbers involved were large or small, conditional offers were used as an additional selection device and the number of offers made was in the order of several times greater than the number of places to be taken up. Offers by Oxford colleges were described as 'realistic' although as many as one-fifth of such candidates failed to achieve the required level of performance. Every Oxford offer had 'a bed to follow it next September' and unsuccessful offers to candidates meant untaken places.

Perhaps it was not surprising therefore that Oxford colleges making conditional offers made no use of S level. Many recorded that candidates choosing to follow this route were unlikely to come from schools which could offer S level teaching. Nor were offers set quite so 'high'. The gaining of an A grade in the subject of special interest was often considered sufficient indication of ability and B (and occasionally C) grades were often recorded as acceptable in less centrally important subjects. Reference was made to O-level grades in some colleges although other tutors expressed reservations about placing too much importance upon them, considering that predictions of A-level performance were the better indicator. In general, perhaps because of the greater involvement in marking and assessing the scripts, Oxford tutors were far less critical of the entrance examination, contrasting 'the ogre of the [entrance] examination ... [and] trying to get A1, A1, A which is too big a burden to impose ... That won't benefit anyone – least of all the maintained sector ...', although tutors were by no means unaware of the need to adapt their process of selection on 'political grounds'.*

Experience of alternative qualifications to the GCE appeared fairly limited in both Oxford and Cambridge. The alternative that tutors were most aware of was the International Baccalaureate. This examination was seen by some tutors as 'very worrying' since it was identified as failing to provide enough depth in the main subject. Where such candidates took the entrance examination the alternative qualification was seen as 'irrelevant'. A few candidates offering CSE – usually in languages – were recorded, often coming from the independent sector. The relatively small proportion of mature students had in general been recently further reduced in response to the reduction of places, although many tutors recorded the value of a few mature candidates in the tutorial system and a number recorded the token 'postman' or 'housewife'. BTEC qualifications had been encountered by a number of tutors but had yet to provide 'successful' candidates.

The final element in the selection process – the interview – although given very different weighting from college to college, was nowhere dismissed as without importance. One Oxford admissions tutor described the interview as 'too flimsy' as a single selection instrument, while confirming that it was 'a useful component' alongside the headteacher's report. Another offered the following order of priorities:

* The Dover committee, whose review of the Oxford entrance procedures overlapped with the concluding stages of this research, has now published its findings (Oxford University, 1983). The suggested abolition of the seventh-term examination and awards and a concentration upon a fourth-term examination with a conditional offer alternative has been ratified by the Oxford colleges.

1. Entrance examination performance;
2. Interview;
3. School report;

and said, 'With all that, one just glances at the A levels.' Although many Oxford tutors confirmed the importance of the interview as a 'trial tutorial' in which they were 'looking for articulate, responsive people' some colleges now interviewed only 10 per cent of the applicants – 'marginals and those seeking places in small or mixed subjects'. The trial tutorial was outlined by one Oxford admissions tutor:

> We begin by trying to put them at ease but quite soon will go on to ask, for example, mathematics or physics questions. For many candidates that's a shock – they have never been challenged to do something in that way in front of someone ... at Oxford the [tutorial] emphasis is on confrontation and interaction ...

Similar interviews were conducted in some Cambridge colleges, with some interviewing candidates seeking conditional offers early to allow 'a second chance' through examination if they were unsuccessful. 'Enthusiasm', 'motivation', and 'subject ability' were aspects which were looked for at interview although not all tutors agreed that there was

> any point in trying to discover academic ability in half an hour's interview ... I don't ask any clever questions [but] prefer to talk about something – anything. I want to see how alert they are, how well they can respond to talking intelligently and sensitively.

A second non-subject based interview was used in some other colleges as 'a slight screening process ... picking up the very nervous, the unstable, the trail of let-off fire extinguishers etc.'.

Some colleges provided guidelines for interviewers; in others there was a standard form to be completed and brought to the subsequent discussion. In a few cases such seeking for objectivity was rather confounded: 'The people I take I just can't help taking'.

Appendix C Material collected in the course of the Project*

Extract from leaflet on courses and entry requirements of a sixth-form college

GCE ADVANCED LEVEL

Advanced level courses are very demanding and students are expected to have achieved good results in O-level and CSE examinations before beginning the course. This means a *minimum* of 4 subjects, preferably above grade C at O level.

In some cases a good O-level grade is essential in particular subjects. Details are available from college staff.

GCE ORDINARY LEVEL

These courses last for one year and students take up to four subjects. It is expected that in certain cases students will already have achieved O-level grades D or E or CSE grade 2.

CERTIFICATE OF EXTENDED EDUCATION

These one-year courses are designed primarily for those students who have achieved CSE grades 2–4.

SECRETARIAL COURSES

Secretarial courses may be taken in conjunction with GCE and CEE courses. The two-year secretarial course leads to RSA examinations in Typewriting, Shorthand and Secretarial Duties. This takes up the same amount of time as two A-level subjects (i.e. 10 hours per week). It is expected that students following the two-year course will have achieved good results in their GCE or CSE examinations and will be following an A-level course here. An O-level qualification (grade C or above) in English language is required.

The one-year courses include Typewriting, Shorthand and Office Practice taught as separate subjects, and students may take up to two subjects. Students wishing to take Shorthand must show evidence of competence in English language.

Students taking a one-year course will choose 4/5 subjects. They will be expected to include Mathematics and/or English language if they have not already gained an O-level grade C or CSE 1.

* Reproduced by permission.

NON-EXAMINATION COURSES

A range of general and support courses is offered, including a variety of Physical Education activities. Students participate in these courses as part of their timetable.

Extract from notes for guidance of referees for completing 1984 UCCA university application form

In fairness to all candidates you are asked to provide information on the topics in the following check list. They represent a consensus among university selectors about the information they find useful.

DETAILS OF THE SCHOOL OR COLLEGE

Insert in the boxes: Type of school or college. Number of full-time and part-time students. Number in sixth form (upper plus lower) or equivalent group. Number normally proceeding to university each year.

INFORMATION CONCERNING THE CANDIDATE

Special features of the school's policy on the taking of O and A level subjects as they affect the candidate. Special or experimental syllabuses taken by the candidate. Subjects studied by the candidate in minority time and not examined. Any special difficulties experienced by the school that may have affected the candidate's performance e.g. staffing or reorganisation problems. In the case of a school outside the UK: in what proportion of courses taken by the applicant is English the medium of instruction?

Academic achievement and potential of the candidate

Please give an indication of the results (grades/bands) you expect the candidate to attain in each of the subjects he has listed; if unable to specify a grade or band give a range ... If neither the actual examination results listed ... nor the predicted results give a fair indication of the candidate's academic potential please say why.

Personal qualities of the candidate

From your knowledge of the candidate's achievement, interests and personality, please make your comments where possible under the following headings:

Powers of analysis.
Powers of expression, both oral and written.
Ability to present a coherent argument.
Imagination, creativity, inventiveness.
Independence of mind.
Initiative.
Industry, determination, perseverance.
Reliability and sense of responsibility, positions of responsibility held.

Breadth of interests including hobbies, sports, involvement in youth organisations and clubs (where not properly covered by the candidate's own statements).

Social abilities and personal relations: contribution to the community (where not properly covered by the candidate's own statements).

Suitability and motivation for the chosen course
Please give your views on the candidate's aptitude for, and interest in, the subject chosen. To what extent is the candidate aware of the demands of his chosen university course and career?

Other relevant factors about the candidate
Please comment on any other factors which should, in fairness to the candidate or the university, be mentioned, e.g. health, personal or domestic circumstances. Selectors may be willing to compensate for under-achievement if adverse circumstances are known to exist.

If, after you have completed and submitted this form, you feel that the information you have provided should be amended or supplemented in any way, you should write direct to the universities or colleges named by the candidate after UCCA has acknowledged the application. (If you do this please mention in your letter the candidate's UCCA serial number and proposed course of study.)

Example of a confidential report used to collect information on applicants to higher education

X Compared with 6th Form taking A levels	X	Tend to X	Average	Tend to Y	Y Compared with 6th Y Form taking A levels
ACADEMIC POTENTIAL Very high ability					Unsuitable for Higher Education
Powers of ANALYSIS Clear thinking; perceptive					Fails to see the nub of the question
Clear understanding					Muddled
Retains facts/principles					Forgets basic principles
Powers of EXPRESSION Fluent; good with words					Hesitant; poor English; inarticulate
Written work well organised					Disorganised
Writing clearly expressed					Poorly expressed
Concise					Rambling; verbose
Well presented, neat					Untidy, illegible
Forceful presentation of ideas					Weak; fails to communicate
Presents a COHERENT ARGUMENT Logical clear development					Unconnected collection of ideas; facts
Can initiate a line of thinking					Can't even follow a line of argument
Shows insights					Little perception
IMAGINATION, CREATIVITY, INVENTIVENESS Original/independent thought					Dependent on fellow students Relies on copying from books
Creative thinking, hypothesises					Lacks imagination
Shows flair for subject					No gift for subject
INDEPENDENCE OF MIND Questions ideas/facts/theories					Easily accepts what they are told
Healthy scepticism					Dumb acceptance
Able to evaluate critically					No powers of critical analysis

APPENDIX C

X Compared with 6th Form taking A levels	Tend X to X	Average	Tend to Y	Y	Y Compared with 6th Form taking A levels
Able to develop rational arguments					Fails to think out arguments

INITIATIVE

Shows initiative in work					Does only the work set
Good background reading					Reads only the textbooks
Follows up with supplementary work					No follow up
Has academic drive					Academically lazy; does not think

INDUSTRY, DETERMINATION, PERSEVERANCE

Works hard; great effort					Lazy
Meticulous practical work; accurate					Careless
Succeeds without effort					Working at the limit of effort
Effective worker					Ineffective
Strongly motivated to succeed					Little positive drive
High capacity for concentration					Easily distracted
Persevering when in difficulty					Gives up easily
Enthusiastic about subject					Indifferent
Consistent progress					Erratic; patchy
Contributes to class					Morose; silent; uncommunicative
Works quickly					Slow; plodder
Presents work punctually					Work always late

PERSONAL QUALITIES
RELIABILITY AND RESPONSIBILITY

Personally reliable					Unreliable; can't be depended on
Mature, responsible attitudes					Immature; irresponsible
Self disciplined					Distracts others
Good leadership qualities					Only a follower
Positions of responsibility held in school					

158 APPENDICES

X Compared with 6th Form taking A levels	X	Tend to X	Average	Tend to Y	Y	Y compared with 6th Form taking A levels
Range of INTERESTS						
Wide interests						Narrow specialist

Interests/activities in school (from Tutor's file)

SOCIAL ABILITIES, PERSONAL RELATIONS

Positive, forceful character	Weak, easily led
Self confident, at ease	Nervous, lacks confidence
Social with peer group; gregarious	A 'loner'
Good sense of humour	Lacks humour
Easy relationship with staff	Too deferential; diffident
Adaptable to H.Ed. life	Rigid; unlikely to adapt
Easy going	Too sensitive; quarrels easily
Will show up well at interview	Will not do justice to themself

CONTRIBUTION TO THE COMMUNITY, SCHOOL AND ELSEWHERE

SUITABILITY AND MOTIVATION FOR CHOSEN COURSE

APTITUDE FOR CHOSEN COURSE – Summary
Has the student the necessary:
Skills? _____
Knowledge? _____
Drive? _____
Interest? _____

TO WHAT EXTENT is the student aware of the demands of the chosen course?

TO WHAT EXTENT is the candidate aware of the demands of the hoped for career?

APPENDIX C 159

FAMILY SUPPORT

HEALTH

PERSONAL CIRCUMSTANCES which should be noted e.g. anything which affects exam results or suitability for the course.

Appendix D Background information

Examining Boards for the General Certificate of Education

The Associated Examining Board
Wellington House
Station Road
Aldershot
Hants GU11 1BQ

Joint Matriculation Board
Manchester M15 6EU

Oxford and Cambridge Schools
  Examination Board
Elsfield Way
Oxford OX2 8EP, and
10 Trumpington Street
Cambridge CB2 1QB

Southern Universities' Joint Board*
  for School Examinations
Cotham Road
Bristol BS6 6DD

University of Cambridge*
  Local Examinations Syndicate
Syndicate Buildings
1 Hills Road
Cambridge CB1 2EM

University of London
  School Examinations Board
Stewart House
32 Russell Square
London WC1B 5DM

University of Oxford Delegacy of Local
  Examinations
Ewert Place
Banbury Road
Summertown
Oxford OX2 7BZ

Welsh Joint Education Committee
245 Western Avenue
Cardiff CF5 2YX

Regional Examining Boards for the Certificate of Secondary Education

Associated Lancashire Schools
  Examining Board
12 Harter Street
Manchester M1 6HL

East Anglian Examinations Board
'The Lindens'
Lexden Road
Colchester
Essex CO3 3RL

* These boards are now linked.

APPENDIX D

East Midland Regional Examinations Board
Robins Wood House
Robins Wood Road
Aspley
Nottingham NG8 3NR

London Regional Examining Board
Lyon House
104 Wandsworth High Street
London SW18 4LF

North Regional Examinations Board
Wheatfield Road
Westerhope
Newcastle upon Tyne NE5 5JZ

North West Regional Examinations Board
Orbit House
Albert Street
Eccles
Manchester M30 0WL

The South-East Regional Examinations Board
Beloe House
2 & 4 Mount Ephraim Road
Royal Tunbridge Wells
Kent TN1 1EV

Southern Regional Examinations Board
Avondale House
33 Carlton Crescent
Southampton SO9 4YL

South-Western Examinations Board
23–29 Marsh Street
Bristol BS1 4BP

Welsh Joint Education Committee
245 Western Avenue
Cardiff CF5 2YX
South Wales

The West Midlands Examinations Board
Norfolk House
Smallbrook
Queensway
Birmingham B5 4NJ

Yorkshire and Humberside Regional Examining Board
Scarsdale House
136 Derbyshire Lane
Sheffield S8 8SE
and
31–3 Springfield Avenue
Harrogate
North Yorkshire
HG1 2HW

National Examining Bodies other than GCE and CSE*

Business and Technician Education Council
Central House
Upper Woburn Place
London WC1H 0HH

City & Guilds of London Institute
76 Portland Place
London W1N 4AA

International Baccalaureate Office
Institute of Education
2 Taviton Street
London WC1H 0BT

Pitman Examinations Institute
Catteshall Manor
Godalming
Surrey GU7 1UU

Royal Society of Arts Examinations Board
8 John Adam Street
London WC2N 6EZ

* For a list of vocational certificating bodies see Locke and Bloomfield (1982).

Regional Examining Bodies

East Midland Further Education Council
Robins Wood House
Robins Wood Road
Aspley
Nottingham NG8 3NH

Council for Further Education
5 Grosvenor Villas
Grosvenor Road
Newcastle upon Tyne NE2 2RU

North-Western Regional Advisory Council for Further Education
Town Hall
Walkden Road
Worsley
Manchester M28 4QE

Union of Educational Institutions
Norfolk House
Smallbrook
Queensway
Birmingham B5 4NJ

Welsh Joint Education Committee
245 Western Avenue
Cardiff CF5 2YX

Yorkshire & Humberside Association for Further and Higher Education
Bowling Green Terrace
Leeds LS11 9SX

Bibliography

ASHTON, D. N. and MAGUIRE, M. J., 1980, 'The function of academic and non-academic criteria in employers' selection strategies', *British Journal of Guidance and Counselling*, **8**(2).

BACKHOUSE, J. K., 1978, *Comparability of Grading Standards in Science Subjects at GCE A Level: a Study of Two examining Boards in 1973 and 1974* (Schools Council Examinations Bulletin 39), Evans/Methuen Educational.

BAGG, D. G., 1968, 'The correlation of GCE A-level grades with university examinations in chemical engineering', *British Journal of Educational Psychology*, **38**.

BAIRD, J. A. B., 1981, 'Industry's knowledge of school examinations', *Educational Research*, **24**(1).

BALOGH, J., 1982, *Profile Reports for School-leavers* (Schools Council Programme Pamphlet), Longman, York.

BARDELL, G. S., FORREST, G. M. and SHOESMITH, D. J., 1978, *Comparability in GCE: a Review of the Boards' Studies 1964–77*, Joint Matriculation Board on behalf of the GCE Examining Boards, Manchester.

BAYLIN, S., 1983, 'South-east pupils fill most college places', *Times Educational Supplement*, 4 February 1983.

BILLING, D. (ed.), 1980, *Indicators of Performance*, Society for Research into Higher Education, Guildford.

BLIGH, D. and CAVES, R., 1979, 'A-level scores and degree classification as functions of university type and subject', in Billing (1980).

BLOOMFIELD, B., DOBBY, J. and DUCKWORTH, D., 1977, *Mode Comparability in the CSE: A Study of Two Subjects in Two Examining Boards* (Schools Council Examinations Bulletin 36), Evans/Methuen Educational.

BLOOMFIELD, B., DOBBY, J. and KENDALL, L., 1979, *Ability and Examinations at 16+* (Schools Council Research Studies), Macmillan Education.

BOARD OF EDUCATION, 1911, *Report of the Consultative Committee on Examinations in Secondary Schools* [Dyke Acland Report], HMSO.

BOARD OF EDUCATION, 1938, *Report of the Consultative Committee on Secondary Education* [Spens Report], HMSO.

BOARD OF EDUCATION, 1943, *Curriculum and Examinations in Secondary Schools: Report of the Committee of the SSEC appointed by the President of the Board of Education in 1941* [Norwood Report], HMSO.

BOWMAN, M. J., SOHLMAN, A. and YSANDER, B. C., 1978, *Learning and Earning*, National Board of Universities and Colleges, Stockholm.
BURGESS, T. and ADAMS, E., 1980, *Outcomes of Education*, Macmillan Education.
CHOPPIN, B. *et al.*, 1972, *After A Level? A study of the Transition from School to Higher Education*, NFER, Windsor.
CHOPPIN, B. *et al.*, 1973, *The Prediction of Academic Success*, NFER, Windsor.
CHOPPIN, B. and ORR, L., 1976, *Aptitude Testing at 18+*, NFER, Windsor.
CHRISTIE, T. and FORREST, G. M., 1980, *Standards at GCE A Level: 1963 and 1973* (Schools Council Research Studies), Macmillan Education.
CHRISTIE, T. and FORREST, G. M., 1981, *Defining Public Examination Standards* (Schools Council Research Studies), Macmillan Education.
COHEN, L., 1970, 'Sixth form pupils and their views of higher education', *Journal of Curriculum Studies*, 2(1).
COHEN, L. and DEALE, R. N., 1977, *Assessment by Teachers in Examinations at 16+* (Schools Council Examinations Bulletin 37), Evans/Methuen Educational.
COMMITTEE ON HIGHER EDUCATION, 1963, *Higher Education* [The Robbins Report], HMSO.
DEALE, R. N., 1975, *Assessment and Testing in the Secondary School* (Schools Council Examinations Bulletin 32), Evans/Methuen Educational.
DEPARTMENT OF EDUCATION AND SCIENCE, 1964, *The General Certificate of Education*, HMSO.
DEPARTMENT OF EDUCATION AND SCIENCE, 1978a, *School Examinations* [Waddell Report], parts I and II, HMSO.
DEPARTMENT OF EDUCATION AND SCIENCE, 1978b, *Secondary School Examinations: a Single System at 16 plus* [Government White Paper], HMSO.
DEPARTMENT OF EDUCATION AND SCIENCE, 1979a, *Aspects of Secondary Education in England*, a survey by HM Inspectors of Schools, HMSO.
DEPARTMENT OF EDUCATION AND SCIENCE, 1979b, *Educational Credit Transfer: Feasibility Study* [Toyne Report], volumes 1 and 2, HMSO.
DEPARTMENT OF EDUCATION AND SCIENCE, 1979c, *Letter to Chairman of the Schools Council: Rejecting N and F Proposals*.
DEPARTMENT OF EDUCATION AND SCIENCE, 1979d, *Proposals for a Certificate of Extended Education* [Keohane Report], HMSO.
DEPARTMENT OF EDUCATION AND SCIENCE, 1980a, *Statistics of Education, 1977*, volume 3: *Further Education*, HMSO.
DEPARTMENT OF EDUCATION AND SCIENCE, 1980b, *Examinations 16–18: a Consultative Paper*, DES.
DEPARTMENT OF EDUCATION AND SCIENCE, 1982a, *17+: a New Qualification*, HMSO.
DEPARTMENT OF EDUCATION AND SCIENCE, 1982b, *Examinations at 16-plus: a Statement of Policy*, HMSO.
DEPARTMENT OF EDUCATION AND SCIENCE, 1983, *Records of Achievement at 16: Some Examples of Current Practice*, DES.

BIBLIOGRAPHY 165

DUFFY, M., 1983, 'Colonizing the Curriculum 14–16', *Times Educational Supplement*, 8 April 1983.
FLUDE, R. and PARROT, A., 1979, *Education and the Challenge of Change: a Recurrent Education Strategy for Britain*, Open University Press.
FURTHER EDUCATION CURRICULUM REVIEW AND DEVELOPMENT UNIT, 1979, *A Basis for Choice*, FEU.
FURTHER EDUCATION CURRICULUM REVIEW AND DEVELOPMENT UNIT, 1981, *ABC in Action*, FEU.
FURTHER EDUCATION CURRICULUM REVIEW AND DEVELOPMENT UNIT, 1982, *Progressing from Vocational Preparation*, FEU.
FOWLES, D. E., 1974, *CSE: Two Research Studies* (Schools Council Examinations Bulletin 28), Evans/Methuen Educational.
FREEDMAN, E. S., 1979, 'The certificate of secondary education and the employers', *The Vocational Aspect of Education*, **30**(80), 73–81.
FULTON, O. (ed.), 1981, *Access to Higher Education*, Society for Research into Higher Education, Guildford.
GARNER, J., 1980, *A Guide to University Entrance*, Ward Lock Educational.
GOACHER, B. J., 1983a, *Recording Achievement at 16+* (Schools Council Programme Pamphlet), Longman, York.
GOACHER, B. J., 1983b, *School Reports to Parents*, NFER/Nelson, Windsor. Windsor.
HAJNAL, J., 1972, *The Student Trap*, Penguin.
HALSEY, A. H., HEATH, A. F. and RIDGE, J. M., 1980, *Origins and Destinations: Family, Class and Education in Modern Britain*, Oxford University Press.
HARRISON, A., 1982, *Review of Graded Tests* (Schools Council Examinations Bulletin 41), Methuen Educational.
HARRISON, A., 1983, *Profile Reporting of Examination Results* (Schools Council Examinations Bulletin 43), Methuen Educational.
HEAP, B., 1981, *Degree Course Offers 1981/82: Winning your Place at University, Polytechnic and Other Institutions of Higher Education*, Career Consultants, London.
HEAP, B., 1982, *Degree Course Offers 1982/83: Winning your Place at University, Polytechnic and Other Institutions of Higher Education*, Career Consultants, London.
HEARNDEN, A., 1973, *Paths to University: Preparation, Assessment, Selection* (Schools Council Research Studies), Macmillan Education.
HENRYSSON, S. and WEDMAN, I., 1979, 'Research in Sweden with regard to predictive tests and interviews for admission to higher education', *Spanar fran Spint*, no. 13, University of Umea, Umea.
HICKEY, A., 1977, *'Qualifying for Higher Education under a New Examination System at 18+'*, unpublished report to Schools Council by ETRU at NFER.
HICKOX, M., 1982, 'The Marxist sociology of education: a critique', *British Journal of Sociology*, **33**(4), 563–78.

HOSTE, R. and BLOOMFIELD, B., 1975, *Continuous Assessment in the CSE: Opinion and Practice* (Schools Council Examinations Bulletin 31), Evans/Methuen Educational.

JOHNSON, S. and COHEN, L., 1983, *Investigating Grade Comparability Through Cross-Moderation*, Schools Council.

JONES, J. E. M., 1983, *The Uses Made of Examination Results and Other Tests, for Selection and Employment*, The British Petroleum Company Educational Liaison.

KING, W. H., 1973, 'A prediction from A-level performance of university degree performance', *Physics Education*, **8**, 106–10.

KIRK, G., 1982, *Curriculum and Assessment in the Scottish Secondary School*, Ward Lock Educational.

LEE, DESMOND, 1972, *Entry and Performance at Oxford and Cambridge 1966–71*, (Schools Council Research Studies), Macmillan Education.

LOCKE, M. and BLOOMFIELD, J., 1982, *Mapping and Reviewing the Pattern of 16–19 Education* (Schools Council Pamphlet 20), Schools Council.

MCDOWELL, L., 1981, 'Regional inequality and higher education in England and Wales', *Higher Education Review*, **13**(3).

MACLURE, J. S., 1969, *Educational Documents England and Wales 1816–1967*, Chapman and Hall.

MANSELL, J., 1982, 'Profiling must be a better way', *Education*, 29 May 1982.

MATHEWS, J, C. and LEECE, J.R., 1976, *Examinations: Their Use in Curriculum Evaluation and Development* (Schools Council Examinations Bulletin 33), Evans/Methuen Educational.

MILES, H. B., 1979, *Some Factors Affecting Attainment at 18+*, Pergamon Press, Oxford.

MILLER, C. M. L. and PAVLETT, M., 1974, *Up to the Mark*, Society for Research into Higher Education, London.

MINISTRY OF EDUCATION, 1963, *Half Our Future* [Newsom Report], HMSO.

MINISTRY OF EDUCATION, 1958, *Secondary School Examinations other than GCE* [Beloe Report], HMSO.

MITTER, W. (ed.), 1979, *The Use of Tests and Interviews for Admission to Higher Education*, NFER, Windsor.

MUNRO, M. and JAMIESON, A. (eds), 1981, *Your Choice of A Levels*, Hobsons Press, Cambridge, for Careers Research and Advisory Centre.

MURPHY, R. J. L., 1979, 'Teacher assessments and GCE results compared', *Educational Research*, **22**, 54–49.

MURPHY, R. J. L., 1980, *O-level Grades and Teachers' Estimates as Predictors of the A-level Results of UCCA Applicants* (mimeo), Associated Examining Board Research Unit, Aldershot.

NEWBOLD, C, A., 1981, *Grading Double Subject Mathematics* (mimeo), University of Cambridge and Local Examinations Syndicate, Test Development and Research Unit.

NATIONAL UNION OF TEACHERS, 1978, *Examining at 16+: A Case for a Common System*, NUT.
NUTTALL, D. L., 1971, *The 1968 CSE Monitoring Experiment* (Schools Council Working Paper 34), Evans/Methuen Educational.
NUTTALL, D. L., BACKHOUSE, J. K. and WILLMOTT, A. S., 1974, *Comparability of Standards between Subjects* (Schools Council Examinations Bulletin 29), Evans/Methuen Educational.
OXFORD UNIVERSITY, 1983. *Report of the Committee on Undergraduate Admissions* [Dover Report], Oxford University.
REES, D., 1981, 'A levels, age and degree performance', *Higher Education Review*, 13(3).
REID, E., 1980, 'Employers' use of educational qualifications', University of Lancaster *IPCE Educational Policy Bulletin*, 8(1).
REID, E., 1981, 'Managers and young employers', *Policy Studies*, January.
REID, W. A., 1972, *The Universities and the Sixth Form Curriculum* (Schools Council Research Studies), Macmillan Education.
REID, W. A., 1974, 'Choice and selection: the social process of transfer to higher education', *Journal of Social Policy*, 3(4).
ROACH, J., 1971, *Public Examinations in England 1850–1900*, Cambridge University Press.
ROBBINS, L., 1980, *Higher Education Revisited*, Macmillan.
RYRIE, A. C., FURST, A. and LAUDER, M., 1979, *Choices and Chances*, Hodder and Stoughton Educational.
SCHOOLS COUNCIL, 1966a, *The 1965 CSE Monitoring Experiment* (Schools Council Working Paper 6), parts I and II, HMSO.
SCHOOLS COUNCIL, 1966b, *Examining at 16+, report of the Joint GCE/CSE Committee of the Schools Council*, HMSO.
SCHOOLS COUNCIL, 1967, *Teachers' Experience of School Based Examining (English and Physics)* (Schools Council Examinations Bulletin 15), HMSO.
SCHOOLS COUNCIL, 1968, *Sixth Form Examining Methods* (Schools Council Working Paper 20), HMSO.
SCHOOLS COUNCIL, 1969, *CSE: Practical Work in Science* (Schools Council Examinations Bulletin 19), Evans/Methuen Educational.
SCHOOLS COUNCIL, 1971, *A Common System of Examining at 16+* (Schools Council Examinations Bulletin 23), Evans/Methuen Educational.
SCHOOLS COUNCIL, 1972a, *16–19: Growth and Response, 1: Curricular Bases* (Schools Council Working Paper 45), Evans/Methuen Educational.
SCHOOLS COUNCIL, 1972b, *CSE: Mode I Examinations in Mathematics: a Study of Current Practice* (Schools Council Examinations Bulletin 25), Evans/Methuen Educational.
SCHOOLS COUNCIL, 1973a, *16–19: Growth and Response, 2: Examination Structure* (Schools Council Working Paper 46), Evans/Methuen Educational.

SCHOOLS COUNCIL, 1973b, *The Examination Courses of First Year Sixth Formers* (Schools Council Research Studies), Macmillan Education.
SCHOOLS COUNCIL, 1973c, *Assessment of Attainment in Sixth-Form Science* (Schools Council Examinations Bulletin 27), Evans/Methuen Educational.
SCHOOLS COUNCIL, 1973d, *Preparation for Degree Courses* (Schools Council Working Paper 47), Evans/Methuen Educational.
SCHOOLS COUNCIL, 1975a, *Examinations at 16 + : Proposals for the Future*, Evans/Methuen Educational.
SCHOOLS COUNCIL, 1975b, *CEE: Proposals for a New Examination*, Evans/Methuen Educational.
SCHOOLS COUNCIL, 1975c, *The Whole Curriculum 13–16* (Schools Council Working Paper 53), Evans/Methuen Educational.
SCHOOLS COUNCIL, 1976, *Sixth Form Syllabuses and Examinations: A New Look* (Schools Council Research Studies), Macmillan Education.
SCHOOLS COUNCIL, 1978a, *Examinations at 18 + : The N and F Studies* (Schools Council Working Paper 60), Evans/Methuen Educational.
SCHOOLS COUNCIL, 1978b, *Examinations at 18 + : Resource Implications of an N and F Curriculum and Examination Structure* (Schools Council Examinations Bulletin 38), Evans/Methuen Educational.
SCHOOLS COUNCIL, 1979a, *GCE and CSE: A Guide to Secondary-School Examinations for Teachers, Pupils, Parents and Employers* (2nd edition), Evans/Methuen Educational.
SCHOOLS COUNCIL, 1979b, *Standards in Public Examinations: Problems and Possibilities* (Comparability in Examinations Occasional Paper 1), Schools Council.
SCHOOLS COUNCIL, 1980a, *Examinations at 18 + : Report on the N and F Debate* (Schools Council Working Paper 66), Evans/Methuen Educational.
SCHOOLS COUNCIL, 1980b, *Secondary Examinations Post-16: a Programme of Improvement*, Schools Council.
SCHOOLS COUNCIL/UNDERSTANDING BRITISH INDUSTRY, nd, *Exams Brief: an Employers' Guide to School Examinations*, Schools Council.
SCOTT, J. F., 1975, *Comparability of Grade Standards in Mathematics at GCE A level* (Schools Council Examinations Bulletin 30), Evans/Methuen Educational.
SECONDARY SCHOOL EXAMINATIONS COUNCIL, 1947, *Examinations in Secondary Schools*, First Report of the SSEC, HMSO.
SECONDARY SCHOOL EXAMINATIONS COUNCIL, 1960, *The General Certificate of Education and Sixth Form Studies*, Third Report of the SSEC, HMSO.
SECONDARY SCHOOL EXAMINATIONS COUNCIL, 1961, *The Certificate of Secondary Education. A Proposal for a New School Leaving Certificate other than the GCE*, Fourth Report of the SSEC, HMSO.
SECONDARY SCHOOL EXAMINATIONS COUNCIL, 1962a, *The Certificate of Secondary Education. Notes for the Guidance of Regional Examining Bodies*, Fifth Report of the SSEC, HMSO.

BIBLIOGRAPHY 169

SECONDARY SCHOOL EXAMINATIONS COUNCIL, 1962b, *Sixth-Form Studies and University Entrance Requirements*, Sixth Report of the SSEC, HMSO.

SECONDARY SCHOOL EXAMINATIONS COUNCIL, 1963a, *Scope and Standards of the Certificate of Secondary Education*, Seventh Report of the SSEC, HMSO.

SECONDARY SCHOOL EXAMINATIONS COUNCIL, 1963b, *The Certificate of Secondary Education: Some Suggestions for Teachers and Examiners*, (Examinations Bulletin no. 1), HMSO.

SECONDARY SCHOOL EXAMINATIONS COUNCIL, 1964, *The Certificate of Secondary Education: an Introduction to Some Techniques of Examining* (Examinations Bulletin no. 3), HMSO.

SECKINGTON, J. M. and REID, M. I., 1981, *Youth at Work*, Royal County of Berkshire, Reading.

SHOESMITH, D. J. and MASSEY, A. J., 1977, *Grading Standards in Mathematics at Ordinary Level in 1976: a Cross-moderation Study*, University of Cambridge and Local Examinations Syndicate, Test Development and Research Unit.

SKILBECK, M., 1983, 'A way out of linger and lurch policies', *Times Educational Supplement*, 3 June 1983.

SMITH, C. H., 1976, *Mode III Examinations in the CSE and GCE: a Survey of Current Practice* (Schools Council Examinations Bulletin 34), Evans/Methuen Educational.

TATTERSALL, K., 1983. *Differentiated Examinations: a Strategy for Assessment at 16+?* (Schools Council Examinations Bulletin 42), Methuen Educational.

TEICHLER, U., HATUNG, D. and NUTHMANN, R., 1980, *Higher Education and the Needs of Society*, NFER, Windsor.

TINKLER, G., 1978, 'CNNS first degrees, entrance qualifications and academic performance', *BACIE Journal*, **32**(7).

TORBE, M., FEELEY, M. and PRITCHARD, D., 1981, 'The uses of English', *Times Educational Supplement*, 1 May 1981.

TORRANCE, H., 1982, *Mode III Examining: Six Case Studies* (Schools Council Programme Pamphlet), Longman, York.

UCCA, 1980, *This UCCA Business*, UCCA, Cheltenham.

UCCA, 1982, *Examinations and Grades. Notes for University Selectors 1982–83*, UCCA, Cheltenham.

VINCENT, D. and DEAN, J., 1977, *One-Year Courses in Colleges and Sixth Forms*, NFER, Windsor.

WILLIAMS, I. C. and BOREHAM, N. C., 1972. *The Predictive Value of CSE Grades for Further Education* (Schools Council Examinations Bulletin 24), Evans/Methuen Educational.

WILLMOTT, A. S., 1977, *CSE and GCE Grading Standards: the 1973 Comparability Study* (Schools Council Research Studies), Macmillan Education.

WILLMOTT, A. S., 1980, *Twelve Years of Examinations Research: ETRU 1965–1977*, Schools Council.

WILLMOTT, A. S. and NUTTALL, D. L., 1975. *The Reliability of Examinations at 16+* (Schools Council Research Studies), Macmillan Education.

WILSON, J. M., 1980, *The Accuracy of A-Level Forecasts* (mimeo), Department of Management Studies, University of Technology, Loughborough.

Members of the monitoring and review group

A. H. Jennings	Formerly Headmaster, Ecclesfield School, Sheffield; Chairman, Examinations Committee; Acting Chairman, Schools Council (Secondary Heads Association)
R. Aitken	Director of Education, Coventry (Association of Metropolitan Authorities)
B. C. Arthur	HM Inspectorate of Schools
J. J. Billington	Deputy Headmaster, High Pavement Sixth Form College, Nottingham (Assistant Masters and Mistresses Association)
W. S. Frearson	Ashford College, Middlesex (CSE Examining Boards)
J. C. Hedger	Department of Education and Science
P. M. Herbert	The Elliott School, London SW15 (National Association of Schoolmasters/Union of Women Teachers)
H. F. King	Secretary, Oxford and Cambridge Schools Examination Board (GCE Examining Boards)
D. I. Morgan	Vice-Principal, W. R. Tuson College, Preston, Lancs (National Union of Teachers)
R. Potts	Harraby Comprehensive School, Carlisle (National Union of Teachers)

SCHOOLS COUNCIL STAFF
K. Weller — Assessment and Examinations Team